ALBANIA

TRAVEL GUIDE 2023

The Complete Guide for First Time Visitors on How to Explore this Beautiful Country & All it Has to Offer. Packed with Information Needed to Plan a Perfect Vacation.

By

Open Planet

CONTENTS

Language & Communication
Useful Websites & Apps

CONCLUSION

INTRODUCTION

I set off on a journey in the summer of 2022 that would forever alter the course of my life. I entered the lovely country of Albania with an open mind and an insatiable curiosity, completely unaware of the life-changing effects this experience would have on me.

When I first came, the vivid energy of the nation mesmerized me. The towering mountains murmured tales of majesty, while the ancient cities rang with murmurs of history. In this location, the past and present coexist peacefully, and I am constantly greeted with friendly grins.

However, it wasn't just the stunning scenery or the varied cultural history that enthralled me. It was the Albanian people themselves, who were strong, kind, and fiercely patriotic. Their tales revealed a nation bursting with untapped potential that was just waiting to be found by the world, shared over cups of robust coffee and hearty meals.

I was engulfed in Albania's hidden treasures as my tour progressed: gorgeous beaches along the Adriatic coast, magical castles situated on hilltops, and charming villages tucked away in the highlands. The more I looked, the more I came to see that this underappreciated treasure deserved to be cherished, shared, and enjoyed.

I made the decision to write a travel guidebook to highlight Albania's treasures to the world after being moved by the country's untouched beauty and unrealized potential. I want to take readers to the country of the eagles with each page and help them see the amazing adventures that are in store for them.

Come along with me as we set out on a wonderful tour around Albania that will leave you wanting more, invigorating your wanderlust, and inspiring you.

CHAPTER ONE

Introduction

Overview of Albania

Welcome to Albania, a mesmerizing treasure tucked away in the Balkans where fascinating culture, rich history, and stunning scenery combine to create a genuinely one-of-a-kind travel destination. In this first session, we'll set out on a journey to learn more about Albania's rich history, delve into its unique culture, and investigate the amazing landscape that has shaped this extraordinary nation.

Albania's history, which spans thousands of years, has been influenced by several civilizations, empires, and cultures. The earliest known residents of the area were the ancient Indo-European group known as the Illyrians. Later, the country bore the imprints of the Romans, Byzantines, Ottomans, and other empires. Albania obtained independence at the beginning of the 20th century, went through a difficult time under communism, and then became a democratic country. Today, its archaeological sites, castles, and museums serve as reminders of its illustrious past.

Albanian culture is a tapestry created from a colorful fusion of influences. The people of Albania also referred to as Albanians, are well-recognized for their friendliness, kindness, and intense sense of patriotism. The culture of the nation is a fascinating synthesis of traditions, rituals, and artistic expressions from Illyrian, Roman, Byzantine, Ottoman, and European influences.

The Albanian language is one of the oldest in Europe, and it is a fundamental component of Albanian culture. Folklore and traditional music, like iso-polyphony, have a rich history in the nation and serve as a means of transmitting emotions and family legends. Albanian food is delicious and offers a variety of flavors that are influenced by Turkish, Balkan, and Mediterranean culinary traditions.

Geographical diversity is as great in Albania as it is in its history and culture. With a coastline along the Ionian and Adriatic Seas and borders Montenegro, Kosovo, Macedonia, and Greece, Albania provides a breathtaking combination of coastal splendor, mighty mountains, lush valleys, and lovely lakes.

The Albanian Riviera beckons visitors looking for a Mediterranean paradise with its immaculate beaches, secret coves, and crystal-clear waters. Visit the historic Butrint, a UNESCO World Heritage Site, or travel to the Albanian Alps, where you'll find craggy peaks, thick woods, and quaint villages.

One of Europe's oldest and deepest lakes, Lake Ohrid is shared by Macedonia and is a calm refuge surrounded by breathtaking mountain scenery. An additional natural wonder worth exploring is the Prespa National Park, which is home to a wide variety of plants and animals.

Tirana, the capital of Albania, is a thriving metropolis where the past and contemporary coexist. Explore Skanderbeg Square, take in the vibrant architecture covered in street art, and take in the vibrant energy of the city's markets, cafes, and restaurants.

The country of Albania is home to a wide variety of attractions that highlight its rich history, cultural legacy, and scenic beauty. Explore the UNESCO-listed city of Gjirokaster with its Ottoman-era architecture, take in the historic amphitheater of

Durres, and see the ruins of a once a major city at Butrint.

The Valbona Valley lures adventurers with its rough wilderness, while the Llogara National Park offers spectacular hiking paths with breathtaking views of the coastline. Be sure to visit Berat, a bustling city also referred to as the "City of a Thousand Windows," where ancient Ottoman homes are dotted around the hillside.

Albania is a fascinating location with a rich tapestry of landscape, history, and culture. Its rich history, which was shaped by numerous civilizations, has given rise to a distinctive cultural identity. There are countless options for exploration and adventure due to the different landscapes, which range from the stunning shoreline to the spectacular mountains. Albania will leave a lasting impression on your heart and mind, whether you're looking for ancient history, real-life encounters, or breathtaking natural beauty.

Why You Need to Visit Albania

Albania is a charming nation with stunning scenery and a fascinating history. Albania provides a variety of reasons to capture the attention of tourists, from its magnificent coastline along the Adriatic and Ionian Seas to its rough mountain landscapes and historic UNESCO World Heritage Sites. The main justifications for visiting Albania will be covered in this section.

Beautiful Natural Landscapes: Albania is home to a rich and pristine natural environment that will wow nature lovers. The Albanian Riviera is a sun-seekers heaven with its clean beaches, turquoise waters, and charming coastal communities. The Albanian Alps offer a stunning backdrop of towering peaks, deep valleys, and flowing rivers for those who prefer the mountains. Incredible opportunities for climbing, trekking, and taking in the tranquility of nature are provided by the untamed beauty of the Valbona Valley National Park and the serene waters of Lake Ohrid.

Rich Historical and Cultural Heritage: Due to Albania's long history, there is a rich tapestry of influences from earlier civilizations and cultures. Discover the historic city of Butrint, a Greek and Roman archaeological site with stunning ruins and a theater tucked away in the midst of beautiful vegetation. Visit Berat, the "City of a Thousand Windows," a UNESCO World Heritage Site with spectacular Ottoman buildings and a mountaintop castle. Explore the mysteries of the ancient Greek city of Apollonia while exploring its monuments, forums, and temples. The history of Albania is a hidden gem just waiting to be found.

Warm Hospitality and Authentic Experiences: The people of Albania are known for their kind dispositions and gracious hospitality. You'll be greeted with open arms, whether you're sharing a traditional raki in a rural village or engaging in spirited discussion over a cup of robust Albanian coffee. The nation provides options for immersion in genuine experiences, including staying in conventional guesthouses, experiencing local cuisine, and taking part in centuries-old festivals and celebrations. Make lifelong memories by embracing the Albanian people's sincere kindness.

Travelers on a tight budget will find Albania to be a desirable destination thanks to its outstanding value for money. In comparison to other European nations, the cost of lodging, transportation, and food is often lower. You can discover affordable lodging that is cozy and where you can enjoy the delectable local cuisine. Enjoy the best of both worlds by traveling magnificently without spending a fortune.

Off-the-Beaten-Path Adventures: Albania is a dream come true for the intrepid tourist looking to visit less well-known locations. With a growing tourism industry, there are still a lot of undiscovered nooks and undiscovered treasures to find. Trek through the Cursed Mountains, take a boat out to the uninhabited Karaburun Peninsula, or see the untamed Albanian Riviera. You'll be far from the masses, surrounded by untainted beauty, and carving a road seldom taken.

Cultural Fusion & Traditions: Because of its special location at the nexus of East and West, Albania is a melting pot of civilizations. Illyrians, Romans, Ottomans, and Communism all left their mark on the nation, resulting in a unique fusion of customs, culture, and food. Discover the vivacious city of Tirana, which is filled with brightly colored structures, active marketplaces, and a booming café scene. Discover the distinctive polyphonic singing, an intangible cultural treasure recognized by UNESCO, and take in traditional dances that capture the essence of the country. Finding out about Albania's cultural blend is delightful.

Albania is enticing because of its stunning natural scenery, extensive history, gracious hospitality, low cost, off-the-beaten-path adventures, and cultural fusion. Albania provides a world of exploration and amazement, whether you're looking for pristine beaches, untamed mountains, historic sites, or real interactions with locals. Accept this undiscovered Balkan treasure and make wonderful moments that will last long after you leave its shores.

Best Time to Visit

The best time to travel to Albania is one of the most important things to think about when making travel plans. With four distinct seasons and a Mediterranean environment, Albania offers a variety of experiences all year long. Each season has its own distinct appeal, so deciding when to go depends primarily on your particular interests and the things you want to do while you're there. Based on your interests, we'll examine the many seasons here to help you choose the ideal time to travel to Albania.

March to May:

Albania is beautiful in the spring as nature rises from its winter hibernation. Wildflowers of all hues decorate the countryside, turning it into a brilliant tapestry of green. With temperate temperatures of 15°C to 20°C (59°F to 68°F), it is enjoyable to engage in outdoor pursuits like hiking, cycling, and seeing historic sites. There is a chance to have a more tranquil and genuine experience along the seaside because of how serene and uncrowded it is there.

Summer (June to August): Summer is Albania's busiest travel period and with good cause. The sun-drenched beaches along the Adriatic and Ionian shores are a significant lure, with typical temperatures ranging from 25°C to 30°C (77°F to 86°F). The waters are inviting for swimming, snorkeling, and other water sports. The resorts and seaside towns are alive with activity, have a thriving nightlife, and host a wide variety of cultural events. The mountainous areas of the interior provide respite from the summer heat and great possibilities for hiking and taking in the pristine natural splendor.

Fall (September through November)

When the summer crowds thin out and the landscapes take on a symphony of warm hues, Albania's autumn is a beautiful season. The range of temperatures, from 15°C to 25°C (59°F to 77°F), makes for a comfortable environment for exploring. During the harvest season, the countryside comes to life with customary pursuits like grape and olive harvesting. Since there are so many festivals and events in the fall, it's a great time to be a culture vulture. Additionally, as the leaves change color, the magnificent national parks provide gorgeous scenery, making it the perfect season for hiking and photography.

December through February is winter.

Albania experiences a unique kind of charm throughout the winter. The alpine portions are blanketed in snow, while the coastal districts enjoy temperatures that range from 10°C to 15°C (50°F to 59°F) on average. Skiers and snowboarders can enjoy skiing, snowboarding, and other winter sports in well-known locations like the Albanian Alps. With festive decorations, inviting cafés, and the opportunity to enjoy the best of Albanian hospitality, the cities have a special charm during this time of year. Winter is a great season to visit historical places and fully immerse yourself in the region's rich cultural heritage if you prefer a more sedate and private experience.

Depending on your interests and the experiences you're looking for, there is no one optimum time to visit Albania. The seasons of spring and autumn provide comfortable weather, fewer tourists, and a variety of outdoor activities. Beach lovers and those looking for a lively coastal scene will love summer. Winter draws fans of winter sports and vacationers seeking a more personal encounter. Albania's rich history, magnificent scenery, and friendly people will make your trip there memorable no matter what time of year you visit.

Albania Travel Guide 2023

CHAPTER TWO

Planning Your Trip

Visas & Entry Requirements

Understanding Albania's entry criteria and visa policies is crucial when making travel arrangements there. You will be led through the information you need to know in this part to ensure a simple and trouble-free entry into the lovely nation of Albania.

Albania grants visa exemptions to nationals of numerous nations, enabling them to visit the country for tourism or business without a visa for a set amount of time. For stays of up to 90 days within a 180-day period, nationals of the following nations are not required to get visas as of the time this guidebook was written:

- Member nations of the European Union (EU)
- The United States
- Canada
- Australia

- In New Zealand
- British Empire
- Switzerland
- Norway
- Iceland
- Japan
- Korea, South

Please be aware that this list is subject to change, therefore before traveling it is always advisable to confirm the most recent criteria with the Albanian embassy or consulate in your country.

Visa-On-Arrival: Albania offers a practical visa-on-arrival option at the airport or land border crossings for nationals of nations not qualified for visa exemptions. Presenting a current passport, a completed application form, and payment of the visa cost in cash will get you a visa for these countries when you arrive. In order to obtain a visa-on-arrival, which permits a stay of up to 90 days within a 180-day window, you must have the precise amount of money in cash, as credit cards are not accepted for visa payments.

Visa Extensions: You must apply for a visa extension at the local immigration office before your first visa expires if you want to stay in Albania for more than 90 days or if you wish to extend your current visa. An application form must be completed, supporting documentation must be provided, and the necessary cost must be paid in order to request an extension. To avoid any problems or overstaying your visa, it is important to start the extension process well in advance.

Work and resident Permits: You must obtain a work or residence permit if you plan to work or occupy a residence in Albania for an extended period of time. These licenses must meet particular criteria and are typically obtained through an employer or sponsor in Albania. The Albanian embassy or consulate in your country should be contacted for comprehensive information and direction on the application procedure.

Validity of passport:

Make sure your passport is still valid for at least six months after the day you intend to leave Albania. It is a common requirement for many nations and will stop any potential problems from occurring while you are traveling.

Customs and immigration: You will have to go through immigration and customs formalities when you arrive in Albania. Be prepared for inspection by having your passport, filled-out arrival form, and any supporting documents on hand. Your passport will be stamped by an immigration official with the entry date, so be careful to double-check the stamp before proceeding.

Respecting Albanian customs laws is crucial because they forbid the import and export of a number of items, including contraband, firearms, counterfeit goods, and cultural objects. To avoid any difficulties or legal problems, familiarize yourself with Albania's customs regulations.

There is currently no departure tax or fee needs to be paid when departing Albania, however, it is always a good idea to check for updates or changes as you get closer to your departure date.

A successful journey to Albania depends on being aware of the visa laws and admission procedures. Verify your passport's validity, research the most recent visa requirements for your country, and become familiar with the required customs and immigration processes. By adhering to these rules, you'll be well-equipped to tour Albania's attractions without encountering any needless obstacles.

Transportation Within Albania

To experience Albania's varied landscapes, thriving cities, and historic sites, travelers have a wide range of transportation alternatives. Whether you're an adventurous backpacker, a family on vacation, or a lone tourist, Albania offers a comprehensive network of transportation options to meet your needs. We'll explore all of the available domestic transportation choices in this section, from roads to trains and everything in between.

Minibusses and buses:

In Albania, buses are the most popular and cost-effective form of transportation, connecting major cities, towns, and even outlying villages. Numerous firms run the vast, well-maintained bus network. Both local and foreign routes converge at the primary bus terminal in each city. Minibuses, usually referred to as furgons, are a common option for traveling shorter distances or to get to off-the-beaten-path locations. Though they can be crowded, they provide a more flexible schedule. The cost of a bus or minibus ride is typically affordable, and tickets can be bought from the driver or at bus stops.

Trains: Although Albania's train network is not as extensive as its bus network, it does provide a scenic and laid-back means of getting between the country's major cities. The country's capital, Tirana, is connected to places like Shkodra, Durres, and Vlora by the main railway line. Trains are a popular option for some visitors since they are cozy and reasonably priced. It's crucial to remember that the train service might not be as quick or regular as the bus service. To guarantee a seat, it is essential to check the schedules beforehand and show up early at the station.

Taxis:

Taxis are a practical option for short journeys or while carrying a lot of luggage and are widely available in urban areas. You can easily find designated taxi stands or hail a taxi on the street in places like Tirana and Durres. Before beginning the trip, it is advisable to haggle over the fee or make sure the meter is running. For the convenience of reserving and paying, many cabs now provide mobile apps. It's advised to bargain a fare with a taxi driver in advance or look into alternate transportation options if you're traveling between cities or over longer distances.

Renting a car is a great way to explore Albania at your own pace if you're looking for flexibility and independence. The nation is home to numerous domestic and foreign car rental companies that provide a variety of vehicles to fit various needs and preferences. Due to its picturesque coastline routes and winding mountain roads, driving in Albania can be a challenging experience. However, it's crucial to become familiar with local traffic laws, as well as the state of the roads, and to make sure you have valid international driving permits.

Ferries are a fascinating method to visit Albania's coastal regions and neighboring islands because of its beautiful shoreline along the Adriatic and Ionian Seas. Between the mainland and places like Saranda, Vlora, Durres, and the Albanian Riviera, regular ferry services run. Corfu and Paxos, two neighboring Greek islands, are reachable by ferry for day visits. During the busiest travel times, it is wise to check schedules and reserve tickets in advance.

Domestic Flights: Although Albania doesn't have a robust domestic flight infrastructure, a few domestic carriers operate flights between Tirana and a few nearby regional hubs, such as Shkodra, Vlora, and Korca. Domestic flights can be a great way to travel more quickly and save time to faraway locations. It's vital to keep in mind, though, that flight frequencies might be constrained and costs might be greater than with other forms of transportation.

Albania has a wide variety of transportation choices, making it simple and convenient to travel around the nation. Albania's transportation system can accommodate all of your travel needs, whether you decide to board a bus to tour its picturesque landscapes, take a train for a leisurely trip, rent a car for flexibility, or board a boat to see its coastline gems. To get the most out of your trip to Albania, keep in mind to plan ahead, check schedules, and take into account the particularities of each means of transportation.

Essential Travel Tips

It's crucial to arm yourself with useful knowledge as you prepare to travel to this fascinating location in order to guarantee a comfortable and happy visit. To make it easier for you to traverse Albania, we will go over key information on money, travel, communication, and regional customs in this section.

Currency:

The Albanian Lek (ALL) is the country's legal tender. It's a good idea to have some local currency on hand, especially if you're going somewhere rural where credit cards might not be readily accepted. Banks, airports, and exchange offices offer currency exchange services around the nation. In urban locations, the majority of hotels, restaurants, and stores accept major credit and debit cards. Cities and towns have lots of ATMs as well.

Albanian is the official language of the country. Although English is not generally spoken outside of popular tourist destinations, you can anticipate that younger generations and those working in the tourism sector will have a basic command of the language. It's beneficial to learn a few standard Albanian greetings and expressions because doing so will be appreciated by locals and could improve your relationships.

Transportation:

There are a number of ways to get throughout Albania, and they are all rather simple:

Domestic Flights: The primary hub for both international and domestic flights is Tirana

International Airport. Major cities like Tirana, Shkodra, and Vlora are connected by domestic aircraft, making it simple and quick to get around the nation.

The most popular form of public transportation in Albania is the bus. They connect towns, cities, and even isolated locations, and are reasonably priced. For shorter trips, you can buy tickets straight from bus terminals or from the bus driver. It is advised to verify timetables in advance because they could change.

Taxis: Taxis can be hailed on the street or reserved through ride-hailing applications, and they are widely available in urban areas. Before beginning the trip, it is advisable to haggle over the fee or make sure the meter is running. Another typical practice in Albania is "shared taxis," which are taxis that have multiple occupants.

Renting a car gives you freedom and convenience, particularly if you want to travel to remote or rural areas. At the Tirana International Airport and other significant cities, there are offices of significant international automobile rental firms. However, be aware that road conditions might change and that city driving can be chaotic.

Local practices:

To have a pleasant experience in Albania, it is crucial to comprehend and respect the local traditions. Here are some suggestions on manners and customs:

Albanians often extend their greetings with a handshake, direct eye contact, and a grin. When meeting someone for the first time, it's customary to introduce them formally by utilizing titles like "Zoti" (Mr.) or "Zonja" (Mrs.) before the last name.

Albania is a country with a large Muslim population, yet it also has a rich cultural history. Although there are no rigid dress standards, it is nonetheless important to dress modestly, especially when traveling to rural or religious destinations. This entails covering shoulders and knees and shunning skimpy attire.

Albanians are renowned for their friendly hospitality. It's normal to offer a small gift, such as flowers, chocolates, or pastries, to show gratitude when you're invited to someone's home. Another custom is to take off your shoes at the door.

Dining Etiquette: It is polite to wait for the host to invite you to sit down before eating in an Albanian home or one of the neighborhood eateries. During dinner, it's customary to keep your hands on the table and to finish everything on your plate as a gesture of thanks.

You'll be ready to tour Albania and participate in its rich culture and traditions if you are familiar with this practical information. Remember that making an effort to learn about local cultures might help you form lasting relationships and have amazing experiences when traveling.

CHAPTER THREE

Exploring Major Cities

Tirana: The Vibrant Capital

The throbbing capital of Albania, Tirana, is a busy metropolis that exhibits the nation's rich history, cultural diversity, and energetic vitality. This international city, which is located in the center of Albania, boasts a distinctive fusion of architectural marvels, a bustling nightlife, and a kind, welcoming attitude. We'll take you on a tour of Tirana in this section, showcasing its major landmarks, regional food, and the finest ways to get a feel for the vibrant energy of the city.

Learning About Tirana's Profound Past

While Tirana's history extends back to the Roman era, the Ottoman era is when it really came into its own. Under communist administration, the city underwent enormous expansion and transformation, and it has since transformed into a thriving hub for trade, culture, and the arts. Skanderbeg Square is a must-see if you want to learn about Tirana's heritage. The Skanderbeg Monument, honoring Gjergj Kastrioti Skanderbeg, the country's greatest hero, is located in this city's primary meeting place.

Architectural Gems: Tirana's streets are home to an intriguing blend of architectural styles. Admire the vibrant structures of Blloku, a hip area that was originally only for Communist Party leaders. Don't overlook the contentious Enver Hoxha Museum, an eye-catching pyramid-shaped landmark from the communist era. With its magnificent frescoes and complex embellishments, the Et'hem Bey Mosque offers a look into the city's religious history. Visit the Eye Pyramid and the Cloud Building for a taste of modern architecture, two distinctive buildings that highlight Tirana's modern style. Cultural Experiences: The National Historical Museum is the ideal location to experience Tirana's vibrant cultural scene. An amazing collection of items, including archaeological finds and communist-era displays, allows visitors to learn about the history of the country. Additionally, the city is home to a number of theaters and art galleries, including the National Theater of Opera and Ballet, where you can see top-notch performances.

Food and Gastronomic Delights: Tirana offers a wide variety of gastronomic options to satiate your taste buds. Albanian cuisine is a delicious combination of Mediterranean and Balkan flavors. A traditional Albanian breakfast of freshly baked bread, regional cheese, and honey will get your day off to a good start. Enjoy mouthwatering meals like "byrek" (a savory pastry stuffed with meat or cheese), "tav kosi" (baked lamb with yogurt), or "qofte" (Albanian meatballs) for lunch or dinner. You may discover a broad variety of hip restaurants and cafes in the Blloku neighborhood of Tirana, where you can fully immerse yourself in the city's thriving culinary scene.

Accepting Tirana's Nightlife: After the sun goes down, Tirana comes to life. The city is home to a vibrant and varied nightlife that offers something for everyone. Start your evening with a leisurely stroll down Lana River's fashionable promenade, which is lined with chic cafes and bars. Visit the Blloku region, which is renowned for its exciting nightlife scene, to get a taste of the neighborhood bar scene. Dance the night away to a variety of international and traditional Albanian tunes as you peruse the city's numerous clubs. The nightlife in Tirana is something you should not pass up.

Tirana is not merely a concrete jungle; there are possibilities to experience nature there as well. At the southern fringe of the city, The Grand Park is a vast green space where you may unwind, exercise, or have a picnic. Another well-liked location with peaceful surroundings and boating opportunities is the Artificial Lake. If you don't mind a little climb, Mount Dajti, which offers stunning views of the city and its surroundings, is only a short cable car ride away.

The dynamic capital of Albania, Tirana, draws tourists in with its fascinating history, stunning architecture, diverse cultural activities, and upbeat mood. Tirana has something to offer everyone, from discovering its unique neighborhoods and delving into its history to enjoying delectable cuisine and taking part in its vibrant nightlife. You'll discover a fascinating fusion of heritage and modernity as you walk through the city's streets, reflecting Albania's ascent into the future. So prepare to discover Tirana, a city teeming with life and limitless opportunities, by packing your baggage.

Durres: Ancient Port City

The interesting location of Durres, a historic port city on Albania's Adriatic coast, perfectly combines a rich past with a buzzing present. Durres, one of the oldest cities in the Mediterranean, has seen the rise and fall of several dynasties, leaving behind a history that draws tourists from all over the world. The highlights of Durres will be revealed in this section, together with its historical gems and the vibrant atmosphere of its metropolitan setting.

Architecture and history:

Over 2,500 years of fascinating history may be found in Durres. Greek colonists established the city as Epidamnus, and it flourished under Roman administration as Dyrrhachium. It served as the Roman Empire's main port and commercial hub thanks to its advantageous position. Ancient ruins and monuments from the past serve as reminders of this illustrious past. The Durres Amphitheatre, a well-preserved Roman amphitheater that formerly played host to gladiatorial combats and other events, is a good place to start your exploration. The Archaeological Museum, which is next to the amphitheater, has a collection of relics that provide insight into the city's early history.

While exploring Durres, you'll come across a variety of architectural styles that reflect the city's various cultural influences. Near the harbor, the Venetian Tower, which serves as the city's emblem and serves to highlight its medieval past, stands tall. Explore the Byzantine Forum, a public space with Byzantine remains with shops and cafes all around it, in the center of Durres. Visit the Venetian Tower of Durres, which provides sweeping views of the city and the glistening Adriatic Sea, for an immersive experience.

Beaches and entertainment: Durres is well known for its beautiful beaches, which help to make it a well-liked seaside resort location. The area's long, sandy beach is lined with resorts, dining establishments, and nightclubs. In the summer, when locals and visitors converge to enjoy the sun, sand, and sea, the Durres Beach promenade is a hive of activity. Enjoy some downtime on the beach, a swim in the pristine waters, or one of the many water sports available, like windsurfing and jet skiing.

Durres features an active nightlife and a variety of entertainment alternatives in addition to its beach scene. Numerous clubs, taverns, and restaurants can be found around the city where you may eat delectable Albanian food and take in traditional music and dance performances. Explore the bustling streets dotted with cafes and stores to get a feel for the city's energetic ambiance. You can also join the residents for a relaxing evening stroll along the promenade adorned with palm trees.

Explore the bustling markets in Durres to get a sense of the local culture there. Here, you can buy anything from fresh vegetables to traditional handicrafts. You may meet locals and try local fare at the popular Sheshi Aleksander Moisiu market, which is close to the city center. Don't pass up the chance to sample Rakia, a well-liked fruit brandy from Albania.

Durres has a variety of festivals and cultural events that highlight the city's traditions and customs throughout the year. The Summer Festival, which features live music performances, dance performances, and a range of cultural activities, is one of the most important events and takes place every July. A wonderfully festive atmosphere is created at this time as the city comes to life with vibrant decorations, parades, and fireworks.

The ancient and contemporary eras of Durres' city center are perfectly merged. It gives guests looking to explore the hidden treasures of Albania's history and coastline beauty a varied experience with its historical landmarks, scenic beaches, and vibrant culture. Whether you're a history buff, beach bum, or culture vulture, Durres will undoubtedly leave a lasting impression on your trip across Albania.

Berat: The City of a Thousand Windows

The city of Berat, which is located in the center of Albania, is a vibrant example of the history and culture of that nation. The enchanting scenery, well-preserved Ottoman buildings, and alluring fusion of medieval and modern elements in Berat, also known as "The City of a Thousand Windows," captivate tourists. Let's explore Berat's beauties and find out about its little-known attractions that make it a must-see place for anyone visiting Albania.

A Look Back in Time

It is clear why Berat received its moniker as you stroll through the city's cobblestone streets. Numerous classic homes with rows of tiny, wooden-framed windows can be found throughout the historic town, which is a UNESCO World Heritage

Site. These exquisitely made and individually designed windows give the city its distinct appeal.

Legendary Fortress: The Citadel

The Berat Citadel, perched on a hill overlooking the city, is a reminder of the turbulent past of the place. This massive fortification, which dates to the fourth century B.C., offers sweeping views of the surroundings. Explore the Byzantine churches, the Red Mosque from the 13th century, and the Onufri Museum within the old walls of the Citadel. The latter is home to a spectacular collection of holy icons painted by the well-known Albanian artist Onufri.

Famous Buildings: Mangalem and Gorica

Mangalem and Gorica are the two neighborhoods that makeup Berat. Mangalem is known for its maze-like lanes and old Ottoman buildings. The slopes are lined with traditional homes that have white exteriors and terracotta roofs, making for an alluring environment for exploring. Don't forget to visit the famous Ethnographic Museum, which is housed in one of these buildings and offers a look into the customs and daily lives of Berat's residents.

The neighborhood of Gorica is located on the other side of the Osum River and is distinguished by its little lanes and stone homes. Gorica, which is well-known for its many churches, provides a serene setting where you may fully appreciate the city's rich spiritual history.

The Holy Trinity Church: A Colorful Kaleidoscope

The Holy Trinity Church stands out as a true treasure among Gorica's numerous churches. Biblical events and local tales are depicted in vivid frescoes that adorn the building's exterior walls. Step inside to take in the ornately painted ceiling and the time-tested but still breathtaking religious art.

The Osum River Is Beautiful In Nature

The charm of Berat is enhanced by the Osum River's winding path through the city. If you're feeling more daring, go rafting into the Osumi Canyon or take a leisurely stroll along its banks. Admire the majestic cliffs, beautiful lakes, and lush vegetation all around you as you take in Albania's breathtaking natural splendor.

Traditional cuisine and raki

Without indulging in some of Berat's mouthwatering cuisine, no trip there would be complete. Enjoy regional specialties like byrek, a savory pastry with cheese, spinach, or meat, and tav kosi, a typical Albanian meal prepared with lamb and yogurt. Drink some raki to wash it all down; it's a typical Albanian brandy that will make you feel good and give you a taste of Berat's culinary history.

For visitors looking to fully immerse themselves in Albanian culture, Berat provides a memorable experience with its architectural marvels, extensive history, and breathtaking surroundings. Take time to take in the atmosphere, see the delicate craftsmanship of the thousand windows, and absorb the allure of this amazing city as you stroll through its streets. The ageless beauty of Berat is waiting to charm you.

Shkodra: Cultural & Historical Hub

Shkodra, an Albanian city in the northwest, is rich in both cultural and historical value. One of the nation's oldest cities, it has seen the rise and fall of civilizations, leaving a rich tapestry of heritage in its wake. Shkodra offers travelers an enthralling voyage through time with everything from historic sites to colorful artistic scenes. The cultural and historical high points of this wonderful city will be covered in this section.

A Historical Walkthrough

Start your investigation at Rozafa Castle to fully comprehend Shkodra's historical significance. This historic stronghold, perched atop a hill overlooking the city and the sparkling waters of Lake Shkodra, provides sweeping vistas and a window into the past. The Illyrians are credited with building the castle, while further contributions came from the Romans, Byzantines, and Venetians. Explore its towering walls to find medieval churches, fortifications, and an Ottoman-era hammam, among other relics of earlier civilizations.

Travel to Shkodra's Old Town, a maze of winding lanes, stone buildings, and secret courtyards, from the castle. You'll come across a lot of traditional Ottoman-style homes along the way that have been transformed into museums, art galleries, and inviting cafés. View a sizable collection of old photos that serve as a visual record of Albania's past at the Marubi National Museum of Photography.

Gems of Culture

Many organizations devoted to preserving and promoting Albania's artistic legacy are located in the culturally vibrant city of Shkodra. Theater plays, ballets, and concerts are presented at the Migjeni Theater, which has the name of the celebrated Albanian poet. Attend a performance and get acquainted with the area's performing arts community.

The Venice Art Mask Factory is a must-see for art lovers. This one-of-a-kind gallery, which is situated in the center of Shkodra, features the artistry of Venetian-style masks, which play a significant role in Albanian cultural events. Observe the detailed details and discover the meanings behind each mask.

Religious Variation

Mosques, churches, and cathedrals cohabit peacefully in Shkodra, a city renowned for its religious variety. The Lead Mosque, a marvel of 18th-century architecture, is one of the most notable structures. Explore its tranquil interior while admiring its magnificent minaret and exquisite decorations.

The Saint Stephen-focused Orthodox Cathedral of Shkodra is conveniently located close to the Lead

Mosque. This remarkable building, which features stunning frescoes and rich iconography, serves as a symbol of the city's Orthodox Christian community.

Delicious Food

Without sampling the local cuisine, a trip isn't complete, and Shkodra is a gourmet joy. The city's proximity to Lake Shkodra guarantees a wide variety of fresh fish meals prepared in age-old, traditional techniques, including Koran fish and carp. For a genuine dining experience, sip a glass of regional wine or rakia, an Albanian liquor, with your meal.

Natural Symphony

Shkodra is a gateway to stunning natural beauty in addition to its cultural and historical heritage. Take a boat tour around Lake Shkodra, the biggest lake in the Balkans, and enjoy the tranquility of the area. Admire the variety of birds that live here and take in the peaceful environment that surrounds you.

It becomes clear as you visit Shkodra that this city holds the key to revealing Albania's fascinating past and dynamic present. Shkodra provides visitors looking for a glimpse into Albania's cultural and historical tapestry a completely immersive experience with its ancient ruins, cultural institutions, religious landmarks, and natural grandeur.

Albania Travel Guide 2023

CHAPTER FOUR

Coastal Delights

The Albanian Riviera

Welcome to the Albanian Riviera, a breathtaking length of coastline that offers the ideal fusion of unspoiled beaches, lively seaside towns, and natural beauty. The Riviera, which is located along Albania's southwest coast, is a treasure that has yet to be found. This section will cover the main attractions of this coastal paradise, from quiet coves to bustling beach resorts.

Beach Exploration: The Albanian Riviera is well known for its gorgeous beaches, where turquoise waves meet sandy coasts. The area offers a wide variety of beaches to suit various tastes. The quiet Gjipe Beach, sandwiched between imposing cliffs, is one beach that must be seen. Only reachable by boat or a strenuous climb, it provides a peaceful haven for people seeking seclusion. Visit the thriving seaside town of Saranda, which is renowned for its colorful promenade and clean waters, for a livelier ambiance. Dhrmi, Ksamil, and Jala are three further well-known beaches, each with a distinct beauty.

Lively Coastal Towns: There are a number of charming coastal communities that successfully combine tradition and modernity along the Albanian Riviera. A small village called Ksamil, which is close to the Greek border, is well known for its stunning beaches and offshore islands. Discover the bustling town center, dine in just-caught seafood, and take in the relaxed ambiance. Himara, with its historic fortress overlooking the coast, is another noteworthy town. Explore the town's fascinating history, wander along the picturesque seafront, and mingle with the kind residents.

Panoramic Views that Will Astound You: The Albanian Riviera offers panoramic views that will astound you. Drive across the Ceraunian Mountains via the mountain road known as the Llogara Pass. Admire the dramatic cliffs, lush vegetation, and expansive views of the Ionian Sea. When you reach the summit, you'll be rewarded with a breathtaking vantage point ideal for taking priceless pictures. Take a boat cruise along the shoreline for a more exciting experience to see the Riviera's splendor from a different angle.

Outdoor Activities: There are many things to do along the Albanian Riviera for nature lovers and adventurers. Investigate the Karaburun Peninsula's fascinating caves, which are home to a rich marine ecology. The beautiful underwater world, teeming with colorful fish and coral reefs, will enthrall snorkeling and diving lovers. The Llogara National Park has a network of trails that wind through virgin forests and lead to secret waterfalls and sweeping vistas, perfect for hikers.

Cultural Gems: The Albanian Riviera is rich in history and culture in addition to its natural beauty. Don't pass up a trip to the historic Butrint, which was founded in the seventh century BC and is now a UNESCO World Heritage site. Explore the well-maintained ruins, which include a theater, a basilica, and Roman baths. Explore the region's rich history at the Ethnographic Museum of Himara, which displays regional customs, antiques, and attire.

Gastronomic Delights: No trip to the Albanian Riviera is complete unless you indulge in some of the region's delicious cuisine. With a meal of freshly grilled seafood, some olive oil that is grown nearby, and a glass of crisp white wine, you may experience the flavors of the sea. Enjoy traditional foods like byrek, a savory pastry packed with cheese or spinach, and tave kosi, a baked lamb dish with yogurt. To celebrate your fantastic coastline vacation, don't forget to drink rakia, a well-known local liquor.

The beachfront splendor of the Albanian Riviera offers visitors an experience they won't soon forget. This area has much to offer for every type of traveler, from its pristine beaches and vibrant coastal towns to its spectacular landscapes and rich cultural legacy. So gather your belongings, don your shades, and get ready to discover the Albanian Riviera's coastline attractions.

Saranda: Gateway to the South

Saranda, which is nestled along the gorgeous Albanian Riviera, stands out as the best entryway to the south. This lovely town is a must-visit location for any traveler experiencing Albania because of its stunning coastline, azure waters, and fascinating historical attractions. We'll delve into the coastal treats that make Saranda a treasure of the southern Albanian coast in this section.

Coastal Jewel

Travelers are drawn to Saranda, a coastal jewel, by its breathtaking beauty and laid-back character. Ionian Sea views that go as far as the eye can see will greet you as you get closer to the town. Pebbled beaches and clean waters offer a serene ambiance that is ideal for swimming, sunbathing, and leisurely strolls along the shore.

The Wonderful Butrint

A trip to Saranda wouldn't be complete without visiting Butrint, a prehistoric metropolis. This UNESCO World Heritage Site is a gold mine of history and is only a short drive from the town. Butrint, which was built in the eighth century BC, is home to ruins from the Greek, Roman, Byzantine, and Venetian civilizations. Explore the historic remains, awe at the impressively preserved amphitheater, and get lost in the intriguing tales of this once-thriving city.

Islands of Ksamil's Paradise

Ksamil, a coastal village with some of Albania's most stunning beaches, is a short distance from Saranda. The Paradise Islands, a group of three little islands, are the main attraction of Ksamil. Take a quick boat ride to these gorgeous islets where you can soak up the sun, go swimming in the clear seas, and have a picnic amidst the lovely surroundings. You will be in awe of the Paradise Islands' serenity and pristine beauty.

Castle Lkursi: A Magnificent Retreat

A trip to Lkursi Castle is essential for taking in the expansive views of Saranda and the nearby shoreline. The view of the town, the Ionian Sea, and the distant mountains is stunning from this medieval fortification perched atop a hill. Take the ideal Instagram-worthy photo, take in the breathtaking sunset, or just unwind in the tranquil atmosphere. There is a restaurant inside the castle where you can eat regional fare and take in the breathtaking views.

The Riviera Boulevard in Saranda

Riviera Boulevard in Saranda is the bustling center of the community. Along the length of the shoreline, there is a busy promenade that is adorned with palm trees, cafes, and gift shops. Go on a leisurely stroll, indulge in an ice cream cone, or locate a quiet area to observe people. The boulevard comes alive in the evenings with street performers, live music, and a buzzing environment. It's the ideal location to socialize with both locals and other tourists.

Foods from the Sea

Saranda offers a delicious selection of seafood specialties due to its coastal location. The neighborhood restaurants provide a genuine sense of the Mediterranean, from exquisite grilled octopus to freshly caught fish. Enjoy a delicious seafood feast while taking in the lovely surroundings and the sea wind. Remember to drink some local wine with your lunch because Albania's vineyards offer some outstanding varieties. The Blue Eye: Nature's Wonder

The Blue Eye, a natural spring that resembles something out of a fairytale, can be found not far from Saranda. A deep pool with vivid blue waters that is crystal pure and serene is this fascinating natural phenomenon. It produces an amazing show and is fueled by a subterranean river. The Blue Eye offers a cool break from the summer heat and is a well-liked location for diving and swimming.

Visitors are enthralled by the coastline scenery, historic attractions, and friendly people of Saranda, which serves as the southern entryway. This lovely town offers a plethora of activities for every traveler, from the historic city of Butrint to the breathtaking Paradise Islands of Ksamil. Enjoy the delicious seafood, soak up the rich history, sunbathe on the beaches, and let Saranda work its spell on you. This coastal beauty will stay with you forever.

Ksamil: Pristine Beaches & Islands

A lovely getaway from busy cities and crowded tourist locations may be found in the hidden treasure of Ksamil. For those looking for a peaceful seaside break, this small coastal community is a must-visit location because of its immaculate beaches and charming islets.

Getting to Know Ksamil

Ksamil is a picturesque coastal community that attracts tourists with its turquoise waters, sandy beaches, and a collection of small islands strewn around the coastline. It is only a short drive from the well-known city of Saranda. Although this picturesque refuge has become more well-known recently, it nevertheless maintains its natural beauty and seclusion, making it the perfect location for visitors looking to relax and take in the peace of the Albanian coast.

coastline of Ksamil

Beautiful beaches are Ksamil's claim to fame and the main draw for tourists. The most well-known and ostensibly most stunning beach in Ksamil is "Pasqyra," sometimes referred to as "Mirror Beach." This spotless coastline features beautiful white beaches and waves that reflect the surrounding lush vegetation. "Pasqyra" offers a tranquil and spectacular experience, whether you decide to unwind on a beach towel or take a refreshing dip in the water.

Along with "Pasqyra," Ksamil is home to several beautiful beaches like "Farka Beach" and "Ksamil Beach." These beaches, with their gentle sands and enticing waves, provide a similar atmosphere of unspoiled beauty. The beaches of Ksamil offer the ideal backdrop for an unforgettable seaside vacation, whether you love swimming, sunbathing, or participating in water sports.

The Beautiful Islands

The group of islands that make up Ksamil, which are accessible by boat or kayak, is one of the region's most alluring features. The "Ksamil Islands," sometimes known as the "Four Islands," are the most well-known of these islands. These little islets, which are not far from the coast, are distinguished by their lush vegetation and clear waters. In order to explore these islands and find remote coves and secret beaches that provide peace and tranquility, visitors can either rent a boat or go on a guided tour.

The Big Island, popularly referred to as "Vivar Kanal," is another island that is worthwhile seeing. A small local population lives on this larger island, which also has a magnificent lighthouse that adds to its allure. Visitors are able to take in the spectacular views of the Adriatic Sea and the neighboring islands by exploring the island's rocky shoreline and hiking routes.

Taking part in Ksamil's Coastal Delights

Ksamil provides a variety of experiences that fully immerse guests in the coastal charm of the hamlet in addition to letting them enjoy the beaches and explore the islands. At the neighborhood eateries by the sea, seafood lovers can indulge in traditional Albanian fare while taking in the breathtaking views of the coastline.

Water sports like snorkeling and diving are popular pastimes in Ksamil for those looking for excitement. Visitors may easily see underwater caves and thriving marine life because of the crystal-clear waters.

In addition, the coastal region near Ksamil has a number of hiking and bicycling paths that let outdoor enthusiasts explore the beautiful scenery and find secret jewels along the way.

A seaside gem, Ksamil charms tourists with its immaculate beaches and alluring islands. Every traveler will find something to enjoy in this picturesque village, whether they are looking for adventure, relaxation, or a combination of both. Ksamil is surely a location that merits a spot on your Albania vacation itinerary with its unspoiled natural beauty, blue lakes, and friendly residents. Discover Ksamil's coastline attractions and make lifelong memories in this enchanting Albanian retreat.

Vlora: Historical Coastal Town

Vlora is a charming seaside community tucked away along the breathtaking Albanian Riviera. Vlora offers a special fusion of cultural heritage and natural beauty. It is known for its rich history, immaculate beaches, and beautiful surroundings. You will be led through the historical marvels and coastal charms of Vlora in this section.

Investigating Vlora's Profound Past

Vlora has a remarkable past that goes back to antiquity. You can see the imprints that various civilizations have left on the town as you walk through its streets. Start your historical tour at the impressive Vlora Castle, set on a mountaintop with a view of the Azure Adriatic Sea. The castle, which was constructed in the fourth century, provides sweeping views and a window into Vlora's past.

Navigate to the Independence Museum, which is situated in the center of Vlora. This museum honors the city's crucial contribution to the war for independence in Albania. The Albanian Declaration of Independence, which marked the beginning of modern Albania, was declared on November 28, 1912, in Vlora. Discover the displays, relics, and images that depict this important historical event.

The Muradie Mosque, a beautiful mosque from the Ottoman era and a symbol of Vlora's cosmopolitan heritage, is another important attraction. Come inside to take in the ornate architecture and serene atmosphere. The mosque, which bears Sultan Murad II's name, serves as a symbol of Albania's wide range of religious practices.

Beach happiness and outdoor pursuits

One of Vlora's main attractions is its beautiful coastline. It's a paradise for beachgoers and water sports fans, with clean waters, spotless beaches, and a comfortable Mediterranean temperature. The major beach in Vlora is Plazhi I Ri, where you may enjoy the sun, a cool plunge in the ocean, and a variety of water sports. The beach has excellent services and a lively scene thanks to the beach bars and eateries.

Visit Radhime Beach, which is close to the town center, for a more isolated and peaceful beach experience. This beach offers a tranquil sanctuary where you can unwind and savor the splendor of nature undisturbed because it is surrounded by dense vegetation.

In the surroundings around Vlora, there are many opportunities for nature enthusiasts to explore. Take a spectacular trip through the nearby Llogara National Park to pass through lush forests, find secret waterfalls, and take in the expansive vistas of the Albanian Riviera. The park is a haven for nature lovers and photographers thanks to its unique flora and wildlife.

Delicious Food and Alive Culture

Without sampling some of Vlora's delectable cuisine, a trip there would not be complete. Discover the town's thriving food scene and savor traditional Albanian specialties with Mediterranean influences. Try favorites like "Tave Kosi," a delectable dish of lamb and yogurt, or "Byrek," a delicious pastry stuffed with cheese or meat. Drink some local Rakia, an ancient Albanian fruit brandy, to wash it all down.

Visit the Historic Museum House of Ismail Qemali to fully experience Vlora's vibrant culture. The first prime minister of Albania and a significant player in the country's independence movement was Ismail Qemali. His life, personal effects, and the historical setting in which he operated are all on display in the museum.

Don't pass up the chance to wander along the vibrant seafront in Vlora, which is studded with charming cafes and pubs and is bordered by palm palms. This crowded waterfront is the ideal place to take a stroll in the evening, indulge in an ice cream cone, and take in the energetic ambiance.

Vlora provides an amazing experience with its blend of history, seaside beauty, and friendly hospitality. Vlora is certain to win your heart and leave you with priceless memories of your Albanian coastal journey, whether you're exploring its historic landmarks, lazing in the sun on its lovely beaches, or indulging in its mouthwatering cuisine.

CHAPTER FIVE

Inland Adventures

The Albanian Alps: Outdoor Paradise

The Albanian Alps are a well-kept secret for outdoor enthusiasts, situated in Albania's northern region. The Albanian Alps offer breathtaking scenery that entices travelers from all over the world with its majestic peaks, verdant valleys, and clear lakes. This section will take you on an investigation of the area's breathtaking natural features, exhilarating pursuits, and quaint villages, all combine to make it a veritable outdoor paradise.

The majestic peaks

The Albanian Alps are home to some of the most spectacular peaks in the Balkans, rising starkly against the sky. The major highlights are the Accursed Mountains, Theth National Park, and Valbona Valley. With their untamed splendor, these peaks make the perfect background for a variety of outdoor pursuits.

Trekking & Hiking

The Albanian Alps provide a vast network of paths that travel through the slopes and valleys for ardent hikers and trekkers. A well-known track that passes through stunning landscapes, deep forests, and alpine meadows is the one that connects Valbona and Theth. As you drive through traditional villages and engage with the kind inhabitants, the tour delivers an authentic experience.

The Peaks of the Balkans Trail is a multi-day trip that passes through Albania, Montenegro, and Kosovo for those looking for a more difficult expedition. The opportunity to experience the area's varied landscapes and become immersed in the local cultures is provided by this trail.

Mountaineering and Rock Climbing

Rock climbers and mountaineers seeking an exhilarating challenge are drawn to the untamed nature of the Albanian Alps. Climbers of various skill levels can choose from a number of routes on the limestone cliffs at Theth and the nearby environs. The steep peaks of Jezerca and Gjallica, which need technical proficiency and alpine knowledge, can be conquered by experienced climbers.

Adventurers who enjoy mountain climbing can set out on adventures to scale some of the highest peaks in the area, including Maja e Jezercs, which rises to a height of 2,694 meters. These treks give you the chance to put your stamina, map-reading abilities, and enthusiasm for high-altitude adventures to the test.

Off-Roading and Mountain Biking

The Albanian Alps are a dream for mountain biking and off-roading aficionados with their untamed scenery and picturesque trails. In the village of Shkodr, you can rent a bike or a 4x4 to explore the secluded valleys, winding mountain roads, and exhilarating descents.

Theth Valley and the Valbona Pass both provide some of the most exciting mountain biking opportunities. Ride your bike through magnificent forests, over wooden bridges spanning raging rivers, and while taking in the expansive vistas of the surrounding hills. Off-roaders may set out on thrilling trips, navigating rugged landscapes and crossing rivers to reach remote regions of the Albanian Alps.

Undiscovered Wonders and Local Hospitality

The Albanian Alps' stunning natural beauty is unquestionably a highlight, but the area's rich cultural history and welcoming people give your travels a special appeal. Visit the historic stone churches and homes in Theth Village, where time has seemingly stopped. Engage the locals; they are always happy to tell you about their fascinating history and cultural practices.

Enjoy substantial Albanian food, including specialties like "flija" (layered pastry) and "tave kosi" (baked lamb with yogurt). Staying at neighborhood guesthouses will allow you to experience the wonderful hospitality of the Albanian people while also providing comfort, home-cooked meals, and the chance to fully immerse yourself in the culture.

The towering peaks, breathtaking scenery, and plenty of outdoor activities in the Albanian Alps make for an amazing experience for explorers. This outdoor haven will leave you with priceless memories whether you're a hiker, climber, mountain biker, or just a nature lover. So gather your supplies, embrace the wild, and set off on an exhilarating trek through the Albanian Alps' interior.

Ohrid Lake: Natural Beauty

For those seeking unspoiled natural beauty, inland excursions are calling. One of Albania's jewels is the stunning Ohrid Lake. This gorgeous lake, which straddles the borders of Albania and North Macedonia, mesmerizes tourists with its glistening waters, verdant surroundings, and historical significance. The appeal of Ohrid Lake is examined in this section, along with its natural beauty, cultural richness, and the special relationship it has with North Macedonia, it's neighbor.

A Natural Wonder, Ohrid Lake

Ohrid Lake, one of the oldest and deepest in Europe with a history that extends back millions of years, lies tucked away among the magnificent mountains of the Balkan Peninsula. All who arrive will be enchanted by its 350 square kilometers of crystal-clear waters that shimmer under the warm Albanian sun. The lake has unmatched biodiversity, supporting many indigenous species and acting as a refuge for a vast variety of plants and fauna. Ohrid Lake has an ecology that nature aficionados will find incredibly compelling, from abundant wildlife to unique fish species.

The Albanian shores of Ohrid Lake are worth exploring because they are home to many charming towns and villages, each with its own special charm. Pogradec, a thriving lakefront city, acts as a point of entry to the lake's Albanian side. Wandering along the promenade allows visitors to take in the stunning scenery and sample regional cuisine at the lakeside cafés. Naturalists are drawn to the nearby Drilon National Park for its pleasant ambiance, beautiful forests, and peaceful springs. Visitors can unwind amidst the beauty of nature, go for leisurely walks, or even rent boats to explore the tranquil waters of the lake.

Cultural Highlights Along Macedonian Coasts

Visitors enter North Macedonia across the border and arrive in the historic town of Ohrid, which is both a UNESCO World Heritage Site and a cultural treasure trove. The town's well-preserved Byzantine buildings, such as the famous Church of St. John at Kaneo, which looks out over the lake from a rocky cliff, represent the town's extensive past. The old town of Ohrid is a labyrinth of cobblestone lanes packed with classic homes, cute shops, and bustling cafes. Visitors can find museums, galleries, and craft stores on the streets, providing a window into the past and present of the area.

Outdoor Activities and Water Activities: Ohrid Lake is a haven for both adventurers and water lovers. Kayaking, paddle boarding, and fishing are just a few of the sports that may be done in its clear, tranquil waters. Visitors can explore the lake's secret coves, remote beaches, and enigmatic tunnels through boating tours. The lake is surrounded by beautiful hiking trails that lead to panoramic lookout sites with breathtaking views of the surrounding area. Ohrid Lake offers countless chances for outdoor excursions, from swimming and tanning to discovering the lake's underwater environment.

Protecting a Shared Heritage: Ohrid Lake connects the natural splendor of North Macedonia and Albania across national boundaries. Due to its enormous cultural and historical importance to both countries, efforts have been made to preserve its distinctive habitat and advance environmentally friendly travel. Collaboration between the two nations encourages conservation efforts, protecting the integrity of the lake and its ecological balance for future generations. By being mindful of the lake's delicate ecosystem, reducing its impact, and supporting regional sustainable tourism efforts, visitors may help with this conservation effort.

Albania has some incredible natural treasures, as evidenced by Ohrid Lake. Its spectacular beauty, which it shares with North Macedonia, exemplifies how nature and culture can coexist together. This inland excursion promises a memorable voyage for those who want to uncover the true essence of Albania's natural and historical assets, from discovering the country's coastline to immersing oneself in the cultural riches of Ohrid.

Gjirokaster: UNESCO World Heritage Site

A trip through time is promised by the alluring UNESCO World Heritage site of Gjirokaster. This charming city, sometimes referred to as the "City of Stone," has a fascinating history, beautiful architecture, and a thriving cultural life that will astound any visitor. This section will focus on the must-see sights and activities that make Gjirokaster a veritable gold mine for tourists looking to get a glimpse into Albania's past.

A Walk Through the Ancient Bazaar

Start your investigation in the Old Bazaar in the center of the city to begin your adventure through Gjirokaster's long history. You'll come across a variety of Ottoman-era buildings as you meander through its winding cobblestone lanes, as well as traditional craft shops and quaint cafes. Experience the lively environment, inhale the aromas of regional cuisine, and interact with the welcoming inhabitants who still live a traditional lifestyle.

Gjirokaster Castle is an impressive fortification that proudly towers over the city and provides sweeping views of the surrounding countryside. This castle, which dates to the 12th century, has seen the rise and fall of several empires and has had a considerable impact on Albania's history. Discover the castle's well-preserved grounds, go inside the Ethnographic Museum, and take in the tower's imposing Ottoman-era presence. Don't pass up the opportunity to attend cultural events and performances performed in the castle's courtyard, which will give your trip a special touch.

Skenduli House: A visit to the Skenduli House is a necessity to fully comprehend the distinctive architectural legacy of Gjirokaster. This Ottoman-era home from the 18th century displays the distinctive stone architecture and conventional interior decor of the city. Admire the fine woodwork, colorful frescoes, and vintage furnishings that take you back in time. Learn more about the local culture by interacting with qualified tour guides who can share their perspectives on the history and way of life of the era.

The Zekate House

The Zekate House is a true jewel for getting a glimpse into the lavish lifestyle of Gjirokaster's wealthy families. Built-in the late 18th century, this beautiful mansion is famed for its elaborate architecture, priceless artwork, and opulent interior. Explore the beautifully furnished rooms, take in the elaborate woodcarvings, and be in awe of the incredible assortment of traditional clothing as you enter a world of opulence. The Zekate House is a reminder of the city's affluent history and offers an interesting look into the lifestyles of the very few.

The Cold War Tunnel: Enter the Cold War Tunnel to learn a secret that lies beneath the surface of Gjirokaster. This underground system was created in communist-era Albania and used as a base for military operations. uncover the communication rooms, wander the dimly lighted halls, and uncover the turbulent history of Albania. For history buffs, the tunnel gives a fresh perspective on the nation's past and a thought-provoking experience.

Traditional foods and celebrations:

A trip to Gjirokaster wouldn't be complete without indulging in some of the delectable Albanian cuisine's flavors. At local restaurants, indulge in traditional fare like tave kosi (a lamb and yogurt casserole) or byrek (a savory pastry), and experience the friendly Albanian hospitality that will stay with you forever. Experience a spectacular celebration of traditional music, dancing, and costumes if you're fortunate enough to travel during the annual Gjirokaster National Folklore Festival. It will awaken your senses and leave you with priceless memories.

Travelers looking for a mix of history, culture, and natural beauty can find a plethora of activities at the alluring UNESCO World Heritage site of Gjirokaster. This city invites you to travel back in time and immerse yourself in the rich tapestry of Albanian heritage with its historic fortress, beautifully maintained architecture, and friendly residents, and delectable cuisine. Get ready to be enchanted by Gjirokaster, where every stone and every tale spoke brings the past to life.

Korca: Cultural & Culinary Haven

Welcome to Korca, a little-known gem tucked away in the center of inland Albania. This vivacious city is a refuge for culture and cuisine, providing visitors with a distinctive fusion of history, customs, and delectable cuisine. Every tourist to Korca is guaranteed an amazing experience, whether they choose to explore ancient ruins or indulge in mouthwatering regional cuisine.

Learning About Korca's Rich History

Korca has a long history and a legacy that goes back to antiquity. Visit the National Museum of Medieval Art, which is situated in the lovely Old Bazaar, to start your adventure. Admire the magnificent collection of religious objects, manuscripts, and icons that illustrates the city's Byzantine past.

Visit the Museum of Education, which is situated in the original Albanian school building, to continue your historical journey. Learn about the trailblazers who were instrumental in establishing Albania's educational system and gain insight into the nation's educational journey.

Strolling Through Korca's Cultural District: The Cultural District is the perfect location to take in Korca's thriving cultural scene. Enjoy a leisurely stroll down Shn Gjergji Street, which is lined with stunning 19th-century structures sporting colorful façade. Explore the thriving art galleries and boutiques that highlight the city's creative potential while taking in stunning architecture.

A magnificent example of Byzantine architecture, the Orthodox Cathedral of the Resurrection, should not be missed. Enter the building to see the elaborate iconostasis and beautiful frescoes that adorn the interior and reveal a bit about Korca's spiritual history.

Enjoying Korca's Gourmet Delights: Get ready for a gourmet adventure unlike any other. The cuisine of Korca is recognized for being both Ottoman and Balkan in influence. Try local specialties like byrek (a savory pastry filled with cheese or meat), tave kosi (a casserole of yogurt and lamb), and lakror (a traditional pie filled with spinach or pumpkin) by visiting the Old Bazaar.

Try Korca's famous beer, brewed with age-old techniques that have been passed down through the generations, to go with your meal. Guided tours are available at the neighborhood brewery, Birra Korça, where you can sample some refreshing beer while learning about the brewing process.

Korca is a city that enjoys celebrating its cultural history via vivid festivals and lively traditions. Plan your trip to coincide with the annual Korca Beer Festival in August, when you may join residents and guests in celebrating the city's brewing heritage. Take in dancing acts, live music, and lots of beer tasting.

Don't miss the Dita e Vers (Day of Spring) festival if you go in the spring. Witness the city come to life as residents celebrate the arrival of the new season with vibrant processions, lively celebrations, and traditional dances. Take in the living environment and the friendly welcome that Korca offers.

Discovering the Natural Environment: In addition to the city's rich cultural and culinary attractions, Korca is home to beautiful natural settings that entice travelers. Put on your hiking boots and set off on a journey through the Gramos Mountain Range. You'll be rewarded with stunning vistas of undulating hills, pristine lakes, and charming villages.

Visit Lake Prespa, a secret paradise tucked away between Albania, Greece, and North Macedonia, for a peaceful getaway. Enjoy a picnic in the midst of untouched nature, take a boat trip on the tranquil waters, and be amazed at the numerous bird species.

You'll take with you cherished memories of Korca's rich cultural heritage, mouthwatering delicacies, and kind hospitality when you say goodbye to it. Travelers looking for an authentic and immersive experience must visit this hidden treasure in the center of Albania's interior.

Albania Travel Guide 2023

CHAPTER SIX

Off-the Beaten Path

Valbona Valley: Hiking & Nature Escapes

For nature lovers and ardent hikers, Valbona Valley, located in the Albanian Alps, is a hidden jewel that promises wonderful adventures. This unspoiled valley, hidden from the well-traveled tourist routes, offers a rare combination of rocky mountain vistas, clean rivers, and lovely old settlements. Get ready to travel off the main road as we explore the beautiful Valbona Valley.

Overview of the Valbona Valley

The secluded and largely unspoiled natural wonderland known as Valbona Valley is situated in northern Albania. Because of its seclusion, its natural beauty has been conserved, making it a haven for people looking for a genuine outdoor experience. The majestic Accursed Mountains serve as a breathtaking backdrop, flanking the valley on either side with massive peaks. As it meanders down the valley, the Valbona River provides a tranquil soundtrack to go along with your explorations.

Trails for Hiking: The Valbona Valley is a hiker's paradise, with a variety of trails to suit all levels of experience. There is a trail out there that will appeal to your senses whether you are an experienced hiker or a casual traveler. The Valbona to Theth trip is the most well-known trek; it's a difficult but rewarding multi-day adventure through some of the area's most breathtaking landscapes. You'll go through thick forests, cross clear streams, and pass by old-fashioned stone homes that dot the landscape.

The trail leading to the Kukaj village is a great option for those looking for a shorter hike. This easy climb gives breathtaking valley views and a window into the manner of life in the area. You will have the chance to converse with friendly shepherds and observe their customary way of life as the trail takes you past meadows decorated with wildflowers.

Nature getaways: Valbona Valley is home to numerous breathtaking natural attractions that will leave you speechless. A hidden gem hiding away in a beautiful woodland is the Valbona Waterfall, so make sure to check it out. The tranquil atmosphere is ideal for introspection and relaxation as the cascading waters create a beautiful spectacle.

The Blue Eye of Valbona, a serene spring hidden deep within the valley, is another must-see site. You can even go for a refreshing swim if you dare in the stunningly blue waters. Make sure to respect it and leave no trace because the Blue Eye is a refuge for endangered aquatic species.

Local customs and culture: In Valbona Valley, the kind welcome of the locals is just as alluring as the breathtaking scenery that surrounds it. Visit the small villages dotted around the valley to get a feel for the old-fashioned way of life in Albania. Get to know the locals, enjoy their homemade fare, and discover their traditions. You might even get the chance to see performances of the region's deeply ingrained traditional music and dance.

Accommodations and Conveniences: Valbona Valley offers a variety of lodging choices to accommodate different tastes. You can choose from welcoming inns run by welcoming locals to camping grounds where you can really immerse yourself in nature, depending on your needs. It's best to pack necessities like a sleeping bag and strong hiking boots because amenities can be minimal.

Be cautious to check the weather before your trip and pack appropriately. The frigid winters and cool summers in Valbona Valley necessitate layering of clothing. In order to successfully navigate the trails, bring insect repellant, sunscreen, and a reliable map or GPS device.

You may truly unwind and reconnect with nature at Valbona Valley, where you can also take in the unadulterated splendor of Albania's environment. This hidden gem is the perfect place for nature lovers and adventure seekers, with its magnificent landscapes, varied hiking trails, and friendly locals. In order to prepare for an exciting excursion into the heart of Valbona Valley, lace up your boots, pack your backpack, and get set to go.

Butrint National Park: Ancient Ruins & Biodiversity

Adventurers looking for a mix of ancient history and natural beauty will find a hidden gem in the southern region of Albania. A UNESCO World Heritage Site, Butrint National Park offers a singular experience by fusing magnificent archaeological ruins with beautiful nature. This off-the-beaten-track location guarantees to whisk guests back in time while engulfing them in the splendor of unspoiled nature.

The Butrint National Park introduction

A large chunk of the historic city of Butrint and the surrounding natural surroundings are included in the intriguing Butrint National Park. This archaeological site, which is close to Saranda, is prehistoric in origin and has layers of history from the Greek, Roman, Byzantine, and Venetian eras. The park, which has a surface area of over 29,000 acres, offers a haven for both history buffs and environment lovers.

Investigating Old Ruins

The captivating ancient remains that make up the center of Butrint National Park are a tribute to Albania's rich cultural legacy. Visitors are taken on a fascinating journey through time as they explore the archaeological site, learning about the various layers of civilizations that once called this place home. Ancient walls, temples, theaters, baths, and a beautiful Roman amphitheater that still stages plays may all be seen as you stroll among the ruins.

The baptistery, an early Christian monument with magnificent mosaic floors that depict historical events, is one of the most notable attractions. The Venetian fortress, constructed during the Middle Ages, offers sweeping views of the park and the adjacent lagoons, bringing a hint of Middle Ages beauty to the archaeological setting.

Butrint National Park is home to an extraordinarily diverse and well-preserved ecology in addition to its archaeological treasures. The park exposes itself as a refuge for nature lovers as you go away from the ruins, offering a variety of trails and walkways to explore. A diverse mosaic of ecosystems, including wetlands, woods, and coastal regions, is created by the park's special location between the Ionian Sea and Lake Butrint.

A birdwatcher's paradise, the park's wetlands are home to more than 200 different species of birds. The park offers many opportunities to see and admire the diversity of avian life, from graceful herons to majestic eagles. The wetlands are also home to numerous reptiles, amphibians, and small animals, making them a sanctuary for those who enjoy wildlife.

The park is surrounded by nature pathways that take tourists through mature woodlands with centuries-old trees including oaks and Mediterranean pines. These routes provide a fantastic opportunity to observe rare plant species, find undiscovered waterfalls, and enjoy tranquil lakes.

Efforts at conservation and preservation

It is crucial to protect the historical and natural assets found inside Butrint National Park. To safeguard and preserve the integrity of the site, the Albanian government, working with UNESCO, has put strict conservation measures in place. To maintain both the fragile balance of the park's ecosystem and the preservation of the remains, archaeologists, biologists, and local authorities collaborate.

Supporting these conservation initiatives and having a truly one-of-a-kind experience are both possible when you visit Butrint National Park. The park offers a chance to discover, investigate, and take in the rich tapestry of history and environment that is present within its confines.

A testimony to Albania's outstanding biodiversity and illustrious history is Butrint National Park. This off-the-beaten-track location offers a blend of historic sites and breathtaking natural features, allowing tourists to fully immerse themselves in an unforgettable adventure. Butrint National Park promises an unforgettable voyage into the past and a celebration of Albania's natural heritage, whether you're discovering the layers of civilizations within the ruins or seeing the unique ecosystems that survive within the park.

Teth: Traditional Mountain Village

Those who are brave and want to experience something real and off the beaten road should visit the town of Theth. Theth offers an idyllic escape into nature and a glimpse into Albania's rich cultural heritage while being far from the crowded cities and tourist hotspots. Theth is a hidden jewel that beckons travelers looking to find the nation's undiscovered gems with its historic stone buildings, beautiful scenery, and kind friendliness.

Theth is situated in the Theth National Park, a stunning wilderness that best exhibits Albania's unspoiled natural beauty. The road swings through rocky mountain passes as you head towards the hamlet, providing breathtaking views of towering peaks, flowing waterfalls, and verdant valleys. Even the travel itself is an adventure that gets you ready for the delights of Theth.

Old stone homes with wooden balconies and slate roofs, which represent the regional traditional architecture, will greet you as you enter the village. Visit the time-defying cobblestone streets and take a leisurely stroll through them. From the ancient Kulla towers that originally functioned as military fortifications to the small church with its exquisite murals, each step brings a new discovery.

Theth is a place where customs have been meticulously preserved. Take advantage of the chance to interact with the locals and discover their way of life. The locals are recognized for their friendliness and hospitality, and they like showing guests about and telling them about their traditions. Join them in their regular tasks, such as tending to the fields, milking cows, or creating customary crafts. Take part in making a substantial Albanian supper while enjoying the aromas of homemade meals produced with ingredients that are grown nearby.

The Grunas Waterfall, an enchanting natural wonder that mesmerizes everyone who sees it, is one of Theth's attractions. Hike along the nearby trails while soaking in the stunning scenery and the calming sound of gushing water. Once you get to the waterfall, take time to bask in its splendor and re-establish contact with nature. A refreshing experience for the more daring is a dip in the crystal-clear waters below the falls.

Some of Albania's most magnificent hiking trails may be accessed from Theth. Get your boots on and start exploring the Albanian Alps to find glacial lakes, alpine meadows, and secret valleys. Panorama views of the craggy peaks and deep valleys that characterize this region can be seen from the Valbona Pass, a strenuous but rewarding walk. For those looking for a shorter adventure, a more accessible choice is the climb to the Blue Eye, a natural spring with stunning turquoise waters.

The Lock-in Tower Museum is an absolute must-see for anyone with an interest in history or culture. This tower's excellent preservation offers a window into the past and illustrates the highland communities' traditional way of life. Discover the exhibitions, be amazed by the relics, and become completely engrossed in the tales that have defined this extraordinary hamlet.

Take comfort in Theth's peace as the day comes to an end. Allow the solitude of the mountains to engulf you as you gaze at the starry sky devoid of city lights. Rest your head in a neighborhood guesthouse, where you'll be treated like family and have a relaxing stay.

With its unspoiled beauty and welcoming people, Theth is a place that everyone who visits is left with a lasting memory of. It is a location where you may get in touch with nature, experience culture firsthand, and escape the hectic pace of modern life. You can see a part of Albania that few people get the chance to see by veering off the usual road and exploring the traditional mountain settlement of Theth.

CHAPTER SEVEN

Cuisine & Nightlife

Traditional Dishes & Culinary Highlights

Albania is a nation steeped in history and culture, and this is also true of its culinary scene. Albanian cuisine offers a wide variety of flavors and classic meals that will please any food aficionado. It combines Mediterranean and Balkan influences. Let's explore the traditional foods and culinary specialties that distinguish Albanian cuisine, from robust stews to delectable pastries.

Byrek is a savory pastry that is a mainstay in Albanian cooking. It is constructed with layers of thin filo dough that are filled with a variety of ingredients, including spinach, cheese, meat, or pumpkin. The layers are baked till crisp and golden, creating an enticing mix of textures. Byrek is frequently consumed as a quick breakfast or as a snack all day.

Tav Kosi is a classic Albanian meal that mixes eggs, yogurt, and delicate lamb meat. The lamb is slowly cooked in a flavorful sauce comprised of flour, butter, and garlic before being covered in a smooth yogurt and egg combination. A hearty and satisfying dish is the end result, which is frequently accompanied by a side of rice or bread.

Fries: Fries are a hearty dish that combines cheese, usually feta or cottage cheese, with peppers, tomatoes, onions, and other vegetables. The cheese is combined with the sautéed vegetables to make a tasty and fulfilling dish. Fries can be eaten as a meat or vegetarian dish and go well with beef or lamb.

Qofte: A classic Albanian meatball, qofte is made of breadcrumbs, onions, and various herbs and spices with ground beef or lamb as the main ingredient. Small balls of the mixture are formed, and these are subsequently grilled or fried. Qofte is a well-liked option for a quick and delectable supper because they are frequently served with a side of fresh lettuce or yogurt sauce.

Baklava: A delicious pastry constructed with layers of thin filo dough, nuts, and honey syrup, baklava is a favorite across the Balkans. The layers of dough and nuts are baked till golden before being soaked in a syrupy mixture of honey and lemon juice. The end result is a rich, gooey dessert that will satisfy your sweet taste.

Flija: Flija is a time- and skill-intensive traditional Albanian meal, but it is well worth the effort. It is made up of numerous thin pancake-like batter layers that are baked separately before being stacked on top of one another. After that, the layers are cooked to create a delectable and savory cake-like meal. Flija can be eaten as a main course or as a side dish and is frequently served with sour cream or yogurt.

Tarator: Made with yogurt, cucumbers, garlic, and dill, tarator is a light and cooling soup from Albania. It is offered cold and is especially well-liked in the sweltering summertime. A cooling and pleasant dish that is ideal for a light meal starter is made by combining acidic yogurt, crunchy cucumbers, and fragrant dill.

The diverse traditional dishes available in Albanian cuisine are a reflection of the nation's history and culinary heritage. You won't be able to get enough of the tastes of Albanian food, which ranges from savory pastries to filling stews and delicious sweets. You can obtain a genuine flavor of the country's culinary delicacies by exploring the neighborhood eateries and markets. This will make your trip to Albania an amazing culinary adventure.

Popular Local Beverages

The rich culinary traditions of Albania are well-known, and the same is true of its beverage culture. Albania provides a vast selection of drinks that are likely to please both locals and visitors, ranging from cool non-alcoholic beverages to distinctive spirits. This section will discuss some of the most well-liked local libations that you simply must sample while you are in Albania.

Rakia: The national spirit of Albania, rakia is embedded in the nation's drinking tradition. The fruits used to make this fruit brandy include grapes, plums, and quince. Rakia is a regional specialty in Albania, with distinct regional variations that frequently feature varying flavors and alcohol concentrations. Rakia is frequently eaten as an aperitif or a digestive and is thought to have therapeutic benefits. It is typically served in little glasses and is best savored with a warm toast.

Raki: Albanian raki is a completely different beverage than rakia, although having a similar name. The entire Balkan region enjoys raki, an alcoholic beverage with an anise flavor. It is frequently sipped in Albania as an after-dinner beverage or as a way to unwind with friends. Raki is often a strong, clear liquor that is best sipped slowly while paired with meze, a traditional Albanian snack.

Boza: A beloved part of Albanian culture, boza is a traditional fermented beverage. Boza is a mildly thick and sweet food that is typically made from maize, wheat, or barley. It frequently has cinnamon or other spices added to give it a distinctive flavor. Boza is typically drunk in the winter and is regarded as a warming beverage. It is a popular option for breakfast or as an afternoon pick-me-up and goes well with typical Albanian pastries.

Dhall: This traditional Albanian beverage is hydrating and refreshing, especially in the sweltering summer months. It is created by soaking barley grains in water, followed by a few days of fermentation. The outcome is a kombucha-like beverage that is slightly effervescent and sour. Dhall is frequently served cold and pairs well with grilled meats and other typical Albanian foods thanks to its tart flavor.

Albanian Wine: Since the beginning of time, wine has been produced in Albania. The nation is home to a wide variety of indigenous grape varietals that yield distinctive and tasty wines. Albanian wineries offer a delicious variety of red, white, and rosé wines, with production ranging from the coastal districts of Durrs and Lezh to the rich valleys of Berat and Korça. Shesh i Bardh (White Shesh), Shesh i Zi (Black Shesh), and Kallmet are common grape varietals. For wine connoisseurs visiting Albania, visiting the country's wineries and vineyards is a must.

Turkish coffee has a unique role in Albanian culture, despite not being a specialty of that country. It is made by boiling finely ground coffee beans in a cezve, a tiny pot. Small cups of robust and flavorful coffee are typically served with a glass of water. In Albania, drinking Turkish coffee with friends is a social activity that is frequently accompanied by animated discussion and story-telling.

These are just a few of the often-consumed local drinks you might get when traveling in Albania. Every sip reveals the nation's rich cultural past and the friendliness of its citizens. Raise a glass for an unforgettable trip to this stunning Balkan country by embracing Albania's drinking customs. Cheers!

Vibrant Nightlife & Scene

The bustling nightlife in Albania is a unique experience. The nation has a wide variety of entertainment alternatives that cater to all tastes and preferences, from the vibrant capital city of Tirana to the coastal resorts of Durrs and Saranda. Albania offers a wide variety of entertainment options, including lively nightclubs, inviting bars, live music venues, and traditional folk performances. This section will show you where to go to get the most out of Albania's exciting nightlife and your evenings.

Tirana: Tirana, the capital of Albania, has a vibrant nightlife scene that matches many major European cities. At the core of Tirana's nightlife, the vivacious Blloku district is home to numerous hip bars, clubs, and lounges. Both locals and visitors can be seen here enjoying the lively atmosphere. For those looking for a chic and classy night out, Hemingway Bar is a must-visit location. It is recognized for its quirky decor and distinctive drinks. Folie Terrace, on the rooftop of a high-rise building, offers amazing views of the city skyline while you dance the night away and offers an immersive partying experience.

Durrs: In addition to being a well-liked beach resort, Durrs in Albania also has lively nightlife. After sunset, a large variety of taverns and clubs that cater to various musical styles and interests fill the waterfront promenade. The beachfront Havana Beach Club is a popular destination for fans of electronic and house music and regularly hosts well-known DJs from around the globe. The Old Town neighborhood has quaint bars where you can unwind and have a cool beverage while taking in the historic surroundings if you prefer a more laid-back setting.

Saranda: Situated on the breathtaking Albanian Riviera, Saranda provides a distinctive fusion of unspoiled landscapes and buzzing nightlife. There are numerous bars and clubs in the city that welcome both locals and visitors. The stunning beachfront location of Mango Beach Club provides the ideal atmosphere for sipping cocktails and taking in the sunset. The main promenade of the city comes alive with bustling bars as the night goes on, where you can dance to a variety of local and worldwide hits till the early hours. Visit one of the rooftop bars with panoramic views of the city and the sparkling Ionian Sea for a more private experience.

Traditional Folk Performances: Albania's nightlife scene includes the nation's rich cultural heritage as well as contemporary places. Traditional folk performances are frequently presented in public spaces, allowing guests to fully immerse themselves in the alluring world of Albanian music and dance. A fuller understanding of the cultural heritage of Albania is provided by the outstanding performances of traditional Albanian dances and music at the National Theater of Opera and Ballet in Tirana.

Safety Advice: It's important to put your safety first while taking advantage of Albania's exciting nightlife. Keep to busy, well-lit places, especially if you're exploring uncharted territory in the city. Take the appropriate safety precautions, such as watching your possessions and refusing beverages from strangers. For a secure return to your lodging, it is usually advisable to travel in groups and use authorized taxis or ride-sharing services.

Every traveler can find something to their liking thanks to Albania's varied selection of nightlife options. You'll be treated to an amazing variety of bars, clubs, and live music venues whether you're in the capital Tirana, the seaside town of Durrs, or the stunning Saranda. A deeper grasp of Albania's cultural legacy will also be gained by seeing traditional folk performances. Make lasting memories while visiting this captivating nation by being safe while experiencing the nightlife.

CHAPTER EIGHT

Outdoor Activities & Adventures

Hiking & Trekking Trails

For outdoor enthusiasts looking for breathtaking scenery and exhilarating adventures, Albania is a hidden gem. This Balkan nation provides a variety of hiking and trekking trails that are suitable for all levels of experience thanks to its rough mountains, clear lakes, and gorgeous coastline locations. Albania has something for everyone, whether you're a beginner hiker or an expert mountaineer. Get ready to discover the breathtaking natural beauty that surrounds you by lacing up your hiking boots.

The Cursed Mountains, also known as Bjeshkt e Namuna

The majestic Accursed Mountains, commonly referred to as the Albanian Alps, are located in the north of Albania. Hikers and trekkers will find heaven among these rocky peaks. The entrances to this magnificent mountain range are the Valbona Valley and Theth National Park. You can start multi-day hikes in this region, such as the Peaks of the Balkans Trail, which crosses Albania, Kosovo, and Montenegro. The trail offers a singular cultural and environmental experience as it passes through alpine meadows, pristine lakes, and isolated settlements.

National Park of Llogara

Llogara National Park, which is located along the Albanian Riviera, is a refuge for hikers looking for a mix of beach and mountain landscapes. A network of well-kept trails may be found throughout the park, winding through verdant forests, alpine meadows, and steep cliffs. The Llogara Pass, a mountain route that provides sweeping views of the Ionian Sea and the surrounding mountains, is the park's main attraction. Any adventurer visiting Albania must hike along the pass.

Mountain Dajti

Dajti Mountain is a well-liked location for outdoor sports and is not far from Tirana, the capital city of Albania. The cable car makes it simple to reach the peak and offers a beautiful trip to the top. After reaching the summit, hikers can take a number of trails that lead to stunning vistas, historic sites, and verdant forests. The moderate Dajti Ekspres Trail leads you through a variety of environments, including meadows, rocky outcrops, and dense beech forests. The effort is worthwhile because of the panoramic views of Tirana and the surroundings.

Riviera of Albania

Along the southwest coast, the Albanian Riviera offers a breathtaking fusion of mountains and sea. This area is renowned for its immaculate beaches, quaint towns, and beautiful hiking routes. A well-known route that passes past magnificent coastal cliffs, undiscovered coves, and olive groves is the coastal trail from Llogara to Palas. Along the walk, there are possibilities for refreshing swims and spectacular views of the Ionian Sea. The Cika Peak Trail offers a hard journey to the Riviera's highest point for those looking for a more difficult adventure, rewarding hikers with panoramic views.

Koman Lake

In addition to being a beautiful location, the Albanian Alps' Lake Koman offers hikers an exhilarating playground. A boat ride on the lake's turquoise waters is a fascinating adventure. Upon disembarking, you can explore the nearby mountains and start out on several hiking trails. A well-known hike that traverses rocky terrain, valleys, mountains, and glacial lakes is the Valbona to Theth Hike. The walk offers a comprehensive view of Albania's natural splendors.

It's crucial to come equipped with the right equipment, maps, and supplies before setting out on Albania's hiking and trekking paths. These pristine locations will also be preserved for future generations to enjoy if the natural environment is respected and any rules or regulations are followed.

For outdoor enthusiasts, Albania is a wonderful vacation because of its varied landscapes and unspoiled natural beauty. Albania's hiking and trekking paths will leave you in amazement and wanting more, whether you're looking for a relaxing stroll along the shore or a strenuous alpine trip. Lace up your boots, embrace your sense of adventure, and take in the stunning beauty that this magical nation has in store for you.

Watersports & Diving

Albania has a ton of chances for outdoor recreation and adventure, especially when it comes to diving and water sports. Albania has plenty to offer everyone, whether you're an adrenaline junkie looking for exhilarating experiences or just want to enjoy the lovely aquatic world. Let's explore the thrilling world of diving and water sports in Albania.

Water Sports: Fans of water sports have the ideal playground in Albania's coastline's crystal-clear seas. There are many different water sports you may enjoy thanks to the perfect weather and immaculate beaches.

Jet Skiing: Experience the rush of speeding over the ocean while admiring the stunning coastline surroundings. Popular beach resort towns including Saranda, Vlora, and Durrs provide jet ski rentals.

Windsurfing and kitesurfing are popular water sports along the Albanian coast thanks to the consistent winds. While expert riders can take advantage of the challenges provided by the wind and waves, beginners can benefit from instruction from qualified instructors.

Parasailing: Fly through the air while attached to a vibrant parachute and take in the expansive views of the seaside. In seaside resorts like Durres, Himara, and Saranda, parasailing is a well-liked pastime.

Stand-Up Paddleboarding (SUP): While perched on a paddleboard, explore Albania's serene bays and coves. Equipment rentals are easy to come by, and SUP is a peaceful way to take it all in at your own speed.

Dive: The undersea environment of Albania is still mostly unexplored, making it a fascinating travel destination. The crystal-clear waters are home to an abundance of marine life, shipwrecks, and undersea caverns, making for fantastic diving opportunities.

Divers of all levels can find a variety of diving spots around the Albanian coastline. Swim among schools of colorful fish as you explore underwater caves and gorgeous coral reefs. Equipment rentals and guided dives are available at diving establishments and schools in Saranda, Vlora, and Himara.

Wreck diving: Marine life has made shipwrecks along Albania's coastline into havens. Investigate the sinister ruins of submerged ships, including World War II artifacts and more contemporary ones. The German submarine U-596 off the coast of

Saranda and the SS Peshkopia in Vlora are two noteworthy wreck diving locations.

Snorkeling: For those who like to stay on land, snorkeling is a great way to see Albania's stunning underwater scenery. You may explore the vivid marine life and rocky reefs just a few meters beneath the water's surface with snorkeling equipment.

Adventuresome divers can explore Albania's underwater caves, which provide a singular and exhilarating experience. For those who enjoy cave diving, the Cave of Dafina, which is close to Saranda, is a popular choice since it reveals amazing rock formations and secret passages.

Safety and conservation: It's crucial to put safety first and safeguard the marine environment when participating in water sports and diving activities. Always adhere to safety regulations, put on the proper gear, and pay attention to professional guidance. Respect the maritime environment by never touching or disturbing marine life and by never leaving rubbish behind.

Prepare to be astounded by the stunning natural surroundings and abounding marine life as you engage in water sports and diving in Albania.

Albania's coastline jewels will leave you with priceless memories whether you're an experienced diver or a novice looking for adventure.

Take advantage of Albania's aquatic playground while keeping an eye on the weather, and consulting local authorities or diving centers for the best places and the most up-to-date laws.

Wildlife Watching & National Parks

For outdoor enthusiasts and nature lovers, Albania is the perfect vacation destination because of its stunning and diverse landscapes. The nation offers a wide range of outdoor pursuits and adventure options, from rough mountain ranges to exquisite coastlines. In this section, we'll look at the fascinating wildlife encounters and enchanting national parks that highlight Albania's abundant biodiversity.

Wildlife Observation: The flora and fauna of Albania are remarkably diverse, with many species being unique to this region of Europe. Wildlife watching in Albania is guaranteed to be a wonderful experience, whether you're a bird enthusiast, a nature photographer, or you're just interested in the natural world.

National Park of Divjak-Karavasta:

Divjak-Karavasta National Park, which is situated along the nation's Adriatic coastline, is a paradise for birdwatchers. The park includes a sizable lagoon and wetland region that serve as crucial habitats for a variety of bird species. Among others, keep an eye out for the recognizable Dalmatian Pelican, Pygmy Cormorant, and Greater Flamingo. Take a stroll in the park or take a boat ride to experience the tranquil beauty of this wetland ecosystem.

Valbona Valley National Park: This park is a must-see for anyone looking for a wilderness adventure in the mountains. This park, which is tucked away in the Albanian Alps, is home to stunning scenery, deep valleys, and crystal-clear rivers. If you're lucky, you might see the elusive Balkan Lynx, brown bears, chamois, and several bird species while hiking across the rocky landscape. Discover the hidden gems of Valbona's pristine environment and take in its entrancing beauty.

Prespa National Park is a paradise for lovers of the natural world and wildlife, and it is located in the country's southwest. The Prespa Lakes and the surrounding mountains are included in this transboundary park that is shared with Greece and North Macedonia. Discover the natural marshes, meadows, and woodlands of the park to see wild boars, wolves, otters, and a variety of birds, including the critically endangered Dalmatian Pelican.

Albania is quite proud of its national parks, which act as protected areas with the goal of protecting the nation's natural heritage. These parks offer breathtaking scenery in addition to adventure and outdoor activity options.

Butrint National Park is a UNESCO World Heritage Site and an archaeological marvel that is located in the southern region of the nation. Learn more about the old Butrint archaeological site's Greek, Roman, Byzantine, and Venetian ruins. In addition to its historical riches, the park is home to a variety of ecosystems, including marshes and woodlands, which are home to numerous plant and animal species.

Llogara National Park is a highland sanctuary with sweeping views of the Adriatic Sea and is situated along the stunning Albanian Riviera. Travel the Llogara Pass, a meandering road that provides breathtaking views of the seashore and the area's natural beauty. Hike through the park's woodlands while keeping an eye out for birds of prey like golden eagles. Enjoy the cool air and get away from the coastal heat during the summer.

Theth National Park is a pristine wilderness that is just waiting to be discovered. It is located in the Albanian Alps. This park is well known for its striking topography, which includes glacial valleys, high hills, and clear rivers. Take on a strenuous journey to Theth, a typical mountain community, to see the Grunas Waterfall's spectacular splendor. Immerse yourself in Theth's peace, and if you're fortunate, you might even see some animals, such as chamois, and bears.

These outstanding national parks were established in Albania as a result of the country's dedication to protecting its natural assets. Each park offers a special combination of wildlife, scenic beauty, and adventure, giving visitors really life-changing experiences in the great outdoors.

Albania's outdoor pursuits and adventure opportunities will undoubtedly leave you in amazement, whether you decide to go on wildlife-watching trips or visit the breathtaking national parks. Get ready for the opportunity to engage with nature in its most unadulterated state as well as encounters with rare and fascinating animals. Albania is undoubtedly a hidden gem for outdoor enthusiasts looking for life-changing adventures.

CHAPTER NINE

Cultural Experiences

Folk Traditions & Music

Albania is a country with a rich cultural legacy, and its folk customs and music offer an enthralling window into the nation's dynamic past and different groups. Albania's folk traditions and music, which range from lively dances to soul-stirring tunes, are an essential component of its cultural fabric. This section will look at some of the fascinating encounters that await tourists looking to immerse themselves in a different culture.

Folk customs:

Rural villages in Albania, where centuries-old traditions have been kept and honored for generations, are the source of many of the country's folk traditions. The idea of "Kanun," an ancient code of behavior that governs different facets of life, including hospitality, honor, and family values, is one of the most fascinating features of Albanian folk customs. Investigating the Kanun and its impact on Albanian society offers a fascinating look into the cultural fabric of the nation.

Visitors can also take part in regional celebrations and customary occasions like weddings and harvest festivals. These events provide the chance to see vibrant costumes, energetic dances, and ethnic music and are a true representation of Albanian hospitality. You will develop a greater understanding of the warmth and camaraderie that characterize Albanian communities by immersing yourself in these joyful gatherings.

Traditional Music: With various regional traditions and influences from other Balkan nations, Albanian music is as diverse as the nation itself. Traditional Albanian music evokes strong emotion with its eerie melodies, rich harmonies, and beautiful lyrics, making it a spellbinding experience for tourists.

The captivating vocal style known as "iso-polyphony," which features numerous voices singing overlapping melodies, is one famous example of traditional music. Local music festivals offer opportunities to witness polyphonic singing as talented singers display their abilities and enthrall listeners with their enchanting vocals. The lahuta (a lute) and çifteli (a two-stringed instrument), two examples of traditional musical instruments, can be seen being crafted at these events.

Consider visiting the city of Gjirokastr, a UNESCO World Tradition Site recognized for its rich musical tradition, to dig deeper into the world of Albanian music. The city is the site of the National Folklore Festival, an annual celebration and exhibition of Albania's traditional arts that attracts performers, dancers, and enthusiasts from all across the nation. Attending this event ensures a wonderful experience and the opportunity to personally feel the exquisiteness of Albanian folk music.

Dance and Performance: Folk dances from Albania are a vital component of the nation's culture. Each region has its own peculiar dance forms that are distinguished by deft footwork, ethereal motions, and vivid costumes. The Valle, or circle dance, and the rapid kaba dance are traditional dances that highlight the vigor and dynamic of Albanian folk performances.

In large cities, there are a lot of cultural institutions and dance studios that offer programs where people can learn these ancient dances from qualified teachers. Attending a dance session not only enables you to interact with the community but also offers a fun, participatory experience that deepens your understanding of Albanian folk traditions.

Folklore and music from Albania provide a window into the nation's rich cultural past. You can develop a close bond with the nation and its people by immersing yourself in the enthralling world of traditional Albanian music, taking part in vivacious dances, and attending vivid festivals. As you explore the captivating folk customs of Albania, get ready to be mesmerized by the beauty, emotion, and authenticity of its cultural experiences.

Festivals & Events

Attending Albania's festivals and events is one of the greatest ways to fully experience the vivid traditions of this country with a rich cultural heritage. Albanians celebrate a variety of holidays throughout the year that highlight their culture's history, music, dance, and delectable cuisine. Participate in these celebrations with the locals to learn more about Albanian culture. You won't want to miss some of the most well-known festivals and events listed here.

International Film Festival in Tirana:

The annual Tirana International Film Festival, which takes place in the nation's capital, opens the cultural calendar. International performers, directors, and movie fans congregate for this important event. Prepare for a weeklong celebration of world cinema that will include screenings of various genres, workshops, panel discussions, and red-carpet festivities. It's a wonderful chance to appreciate the craft of filmmaking and see how Albania's budding film industry is producing new talent.

Gjirokastr National Folklore Festival: Visit the old city of Gjirokastr during the National Folklore Festival for a wholly genuine cultural experience. International performers as well as folk dance and music ensembles from throughout Albania participate in this biennial event. Watch riveting performances of folk dances, take in the heartfelt folk tunes, and be amazed by the vibrant costumes. Additionally, the event offers workshops, exhibitions, and craft fairs where you may discover traditional Albanian handicrafts.

Kruja Ethnographic Festival: Kruja, a town known for its historical value and traditional crafts, is held close to the capital. The Kruja Ethnographic Festival, a celebration of Albanian heritage, is held there each July. Take a stroll around the winding cobblestone alleyways and stop by the bustling bazaar where craftspeople are displaying their abilities in weaving, woodcarving, and pottery. A local folklore ensemble will be performing, presenting their cultural customs through dance and music.

Albanian Riviera Music Festival: If you enjoy music, you won't want to miss the Albanian Riviera Music Festival. This festival, which takes place in the charming coastal town of Saranda, has a wide range of regional and international performers. The stages come alive with enthralling performances against the backdrop of the turquoise Adriatic Sea, ranging from jazz and rock to traditional Albanian music. Put yourself in a lively environment and allow the music of Albania to move you.

National Independence Day: On November 28, Albania commemorates the date that it gained independence from Ottoman domination in 1912. Parades, concerts, and fireworks light up the city as it transforms into a hub of celebrations in Tirana, the capital. Join the community in saluting the nation's heroes and raising the Albanian flag and singing patriotic songs. It's a significant event that unites people and promotes a sense of pride and unity.

Keep in mind to double-check the precise dates and information for these celebrations and events as they may change from year to year. Attending these cultural events will not only give you priceless memories but will also help you better understand and appreciate Albania's rich cultural history.

Be sure to interact with people, sample local cuisine, and catch the essence of Albania's vibrant cultural tapestry as you visit the country's festivals and events. These encounters will surely improve your trip and give you a deep appreciation for Albania's cultural traditions' richness and diversity.

Arts & Crafts

The flourishing arts and crafts industry in Albania is a reflection of its rich cultural past. The nation offers a unique mix of artistic pursuits that are sure to enthrall visitors, from ancient traditions to modern manifestations. This section will discuss some of the most noteworthy arts and crafts activities you can take advantage of when traveling to Albania.

Traditional Arts & Crafts: Albania has a rich tradition of traditional arts and crafts, with artists retaining old methods and passing them down through the generations. The delicate metalwork known as filigree, which is made by painstakingly twisting and forming silver or gold wires to create beautiful designs, is one of the most well-known crafts. In the markets and workshops of cities like Tirana and Berat, you may discover magnificent filigree jewelry such as earrings, necklaces, and bracelets.

Rug weaving is another age-old art form with a rich cultural history in Albania. Traditional looms are used by expert weavers to produce colorful, handwoven rugs and carpets that include complex patterns and designs. Rugs are particularly well-known for being produced in the city of Shkodra, and you can visit nearby workshops to see the weaving process in action and perhaps buy a one-of-a-kind rug as a souvenir.

Contemporary Art: In recent years, Albania's contemporary art scene has developed as artists have pushed limits and investigated fresh modes of expression. For art lovers, the National Gallery of Arts in Tirana is a must-visit location as it houses a varied collection of Albanian artwork from various eras. Paintings, sculptures, and installations that provide insights into the history of the nation and the perspectives of its artists are on display in the gallery.

Visit the alternative art spaces and galleries that have sprung up in locations like Tirana and Shkodra for a more immersive experience. These venues regularly feature performances, exhibitions, and interactive artworks, giving both national and international artists a platform to present their work and interact with the audience. Watch the local art scene to learn about upcoming performances and exhibits.

Folk music and culture

Folklore and music are incredibly important to Albanian culture. Traditional music has been designated as a component of humanity's Intangible Cultural Heritage by UNESCO, such as the multipart singing style known as iso-polyphony. Attending neighborhood festivals or traditional music performances will allow you to directly experience the power of iso-polyphony. You will get carried away into the heart of Albanian culture by the ethereally lovely harmonies and rhythms.

Visit one of the many ethnographic museums spread out around the nation if you're interested in learning more about traditional dance and attire. By showcasing traditional attire, musical instruments, and objects that demonstrate the cultural diversity and historical importance of Albanian folklore, these museums offer a window into the past.

A compelling fusion of history and innovation may be found in Albania's arts & crafts scene. You'll find a nation full of cultural experiences whether you explore traditional skills like filigree and rug weaving or immerse yourself in modern art and music. Albania invites you to take in the creativity and craftsmanship that have defined its identity, from the vibrant markets to the galleries and performances. Accept the chance to interact with regional artisans and artists, and bring something from Albania with you as a treasured souvenir of your trip.

CHAPTER TEN

Practical Information

Accommodation Options

With its breathtaking scenery, extensive history, and vibrant culture, Albania is a popular tourist destination. Finding the ideal lodging is crucial for a memorable visit, regardless of whether you're organizing a leisurely beach vacation, an action-packed mountain climb, or a cultural exploration of ancient ruins. This section will walk you through Albania's wide variety of lodging options, which may be tailored to suit various needs and interests.

Hotels: Albania offers a variety of lodging options, from opulent five-star hotels to quaint boutique properties and reasonably priced alternatives. There are numerous well-known worldwide chain hotels in major towns like Tirana, Durres, and Vlora that offer upmarket amenities and services. These hotels frequently provide contemporary accommodations, on-site dining options, exercise centers, spas, and meeting spaces. English-speaking staff, free Wi-Fi, and easy access to neighboring attractions are all to be expected.

Boutique hotels and guesthouses are excellent options for individuals looking for a more genuine experience. These smaller businesses are frequently owned by families and offer individualized service in a welcoming environment. Many boutique hotels are housed in old structures, including restored Ottoman houses, giving your stay a unique charm. These lodgings can be found in both urban and rural settings, letting you get a real sense of the people and their customs.

Hostels:

Hostels are widely available in Albania and are perfect for tourists on a tight budget and backpackers. They provide private rooms for people who prefer more privacy as well as reasonably priced dormitory-style lodging. Hostels offer the opportunity to interact with other tourists in shared common areas, public kitchens, and planned events in addition to being cost-effective. Most hostels are in convenient locations that make it simple to visit neighboring landmarks and connect with other explorers.

Bed and breakfasts and guesthouses: These lodging types are well-liked choices for tourists seeking a more individualized and intimate experience. These lodgings are often smaller, family-run establishments that provide cozy rooms and home-cooked meals. When you stay in a guesthouse or bed and breakfast, you can connect intimately with the owners, who frequently know the area well and can offer advice and insider information. Many guesthouses are found in beautiful areas with beautiful views and convenient access to outdoor activities.

vacation Apartments and Villas: Renting a vacation apartment or villa can be a great option if you're considering an extended stay or traveling in a group. Albania has a variety of self-catering lodging options, including cozy flats in crowded towns and roomy villas tucked away in peaceful coastal or alpine places. These choices offer all the conveniences of a home, such as fully furnished kitchens, living rooms, and private outdoor areas. Renting an apartment or villa gives you the freedom to experience local culture firsthand, shop at neighboring markets, and travel at your own speed.

Camping and glamping: Albania offers a variety of camping and glamping (glamorous camping) opportunities for outdoor enthusiasts and thrill seekers. Outdoor enthusiasts have plenty of options thanks to the gorgeous landscapes of the nation, which include national parks, immaculate beaches, and mountain ranges. Basic amenities like restrooms, showers, and occasionally even power are frequently available at campgrounds. Contrarily, glamping locations provide a more opulent camping experience with plush beds, chic decor, and extras like private toilets and outdoor dining spaces. You can fully experience Albania's natural splendor by camping or glamping, awakening to breathtaking views, and exploring the great outdoors.

When selecting your lodging for your vacation to Albania, take into account your tastes, budget, and intended experiences. Albania offers a variety of accommodations to meet the needs of any traveler, whether you choose an opulent hotel, a welcoming guesthouse, or picturesque camping. Remember to reserve ahead of time, especially during busy travel times, to guarantee your favorite lodging and maximize your time in this fascinating nation.

Safety Tips & Emergencies

Albania is a lovely, hospitable nation with a fascinating past and magnificent scenery. The importance of putting safety first and being ready for emergencies cannot be overstated when visiting any location. You may make sure that your trip through Albania goes smoothly and is pleasurable by adhering to this safety advice and recommendations.

Safety precautions in general:

- By often monitoring travel warnings and local news sources, you can keep up with the most recent developments in Albania.
- Keep a copy of any critical documents, including your passport, identity, and travel insurance, or scan them digitally. Keep them apart from the originals in a safe place.
- When touring new places, especially at night, use caution. Remain in bright, populated locations.
- To reduce the chance of theft, stay away from flaunting pricey jewelry, cameras, or other equipment in public areas.
- Especially in crowded tourist places and while riding public transportation, keep your items close at hand.

- Trust your instincts and contact the local authorities or your lodging if you notice any strange behavior or feel unsafe.

Transportation Safety:

- Use only authorized taxis or reliable ride-sharing services for your transportation. Before entering the vehicle, check the fare and make sure the meter is running.
- If you intend to drive in Albania, become familiar with the country's traffic regulations and road conditions. Be extra careful on mountain roads, which can be congested and twisty.
- Be mindful of your surroundings and keep a watch on your valuables when utilizing public transportation. Keep expensive objects and huge sums of money out of sight.

Natural Hazards:

- Because of Albania's earthquake vulnerability, it's crucial to become aware of the earthquake safety measures that your lodging will provide. Locate safe areas and emergency exits in structures.

- Always check the weather and terrain before going on a hike or exploring a natural area. Share your plans and expected return time with someone.
- Forest fires should be avoided in the summer. Avoid starting fires in unapproved places and heed any instructions or warnings from local authorities.

Health and Medical Emergencies:

- Make sure you have comprehensive travel insurance that covers medical costs, including emergency evacuation if necessary, before you depart for Albania.
- Fill a basic first aid box with necessary items, such as any personal prescriptions you might need.
- Find out where the nearest pharmacies, medical facilities, and hospitals are located. Albania's emergency phone number is 112.
- To prevent waterborne infections, use bottled water or take water purification tablets. In addition, be cautious while eating food from street vendors and make sure it is freshly prepared and served hot.

Cultural considerations:

- Be respectful of Albanian traditions and customs. When visiting religious sites, dress modestly and adhere to any instructions given.
- Be careful when taking pictures or videos of residents, especially in rural regions. Always get consent because some people can feel uncomfortable having their image taken.

You can enjoy a memorable and risk-free trip to Albania by heeding this safety advice and being ready for eventualities. Don't forget to exercise common sense, be on the lookout for danger, and accept the warm hospitality of the Albanian people.

Language & Communication

Any trip must include language learning, and Albania is no exception. The Albanian language is distinctive and plays a significant role in the national culture. The Albanian language and its distinctive features will be covered in this section, along with some helpful words and pointers to help you communicate more effectively when visiting Albania.

The language of Albania:

The majority of people in Albania speak Albanian, which is also its official language. Albanian is not related to any other major European language because it is an Indo-European language with its own unique branch. Its two primary dialects are Tosk in the south and Gheg in the north. Despite considerable differences in sound and vocabulary, Gheg and Tosk are mutually understandable.

Basic Expressions

Your vacation experience will be much improved and you'll be able to interact with the people if you learn a few basic Albanian phrases. Here are some crucial keywords to get you kick-started:

- Hey: Përshëndetje (Pur-shen-det-yeh)
- Thank you: Faleminderit (Fa-le-min-deh-reet)
- Yes: Po (Poh)
- No: Jo (Yoh)
- Excuse me: Më falni (Muh fahl-nee)
- Farewell: Mirupafshim (Meer-oo-pahf-sheem)

English Fluency: Many people, especially younger age, speak English in tourist areas, hotels, and restaurants. Learning some fundamental Albanian words is still advised, both as a courtesy and to make it easier to communicate in more rural or distant places where English skills may be weak.

Gestures and body language: Albanians are typically sociable and outgoing, and their culture places a high value on nonverbal communication. The universal expressions of appreciation and friendship are a grin and a nod. To prevent miscommunication, it's crucial to be aware of cultural variations in body language. For instance, it's preferable to point with your open hand when indicating directions or items rather than your index finger, which is seen as disrespectful.

Language applications and Resources: You can use language learning applications like Duolingo, Babbel, or Memrise, which provide courses in Albanian, to develop your language abilities. When you run into language obstacles, having a pocket-sized Albanian phrasebook or using translation tools like Google Translate can be helpful.

Respecting Cultural Exchange: Acquiring a basic command of the native tongue demonstrates an understanding of and respect for Albanian culture. Locals frequently appreciate tourists who try to converse in Albanian, even if it's just to say hello. A deeper understanding of the nation and its people can result from this straightforward action.

Language Barriers: Although the Albanian language may appear difficult to non-native speakers, don't give up. The natives are usually understanding and patient, and they will respect your attempt to communicate. Even if you have trouble pronouncing words or make errors, your willingness to try will be appreciated.

Connecting with Albania's people and culture requires a strong command of the language and effective communication. You can improve your trip experience and develop closer ties with the hospitable Albanian people by picking up a few useful words and studying the native tongue.

Useful Websites & Apps

Having access to trustworthy information and practical tools can significantly improve your travel experience in the digital era. A gem of the Balkans, Albania provides a wide variety of thrilling activities, a dynamic culture, and magnificent scenery. Here are some crucial websites and apps that will enable you to efficiently travel the nation and make the most of your trip.

VisitAlbania.com:

The official tourism website of Albania, VisitAlbania.com, should be one of your first stops online. You can get in-depth information on the many states, cities, tourist destinations, and lodging options right here. The website provides comprehensive itineraries, travel suggestions, and useful guidance to assist you in planning your trip. You can also find future celebrations, events, and cultural activities that can fit with your stay.

Mobile tourism app for Albania:

Consider downloading the Albania Tourism mobile app if you'd want to have useful travel information at your fingertips. This app, which is accessible on both iOS and Android, offers a plethora of information about the nation's tourist attractions, historical sites, natural wonders, and leisure opportunities. It provides interactive maps, suggested routes, and useful details on travel, lodging, and neighborhood amenities. You may save your favorite locations and make custom travel itineraries with the app.

Google Maps: While traveling in Albania, Google Maps might come in quite handy as a reliable navigation tool. It offers numerous transportation options, real-time traffic data, and precise directions. Google Maps will direct you to your preferred locations whether you're walking, driving, or taking public transportation. The app also provides useful details about surrounding eateries, lodging options, tourist sites, and user reviews to help you plan your trip with confidence.

Albania Xplore

Xplore Albania is a fantastic resource for outdoor enthusiasts and those looking for adventure. Their website and app are dedicated to promoting ecotourism and disseminating details about outdoor pursuits, hiking routes, national parks, and other Albanian natural beauties. Whether you want to hike across the Albanian Alps, find undiscovered caverns, or visit pristine beaches, Xplore Albania offers a comprehensive guidebook and professional assistance for life-changing excursions.

Both Airbnb and Booking.com:

Booking.com and Airbnb are two well-known websites that provide a variety of lodging options in Albania. You can easily compare prices, read reviews, and make reservations using Booking.com's wide range of hotels, guesthouses, and hostels. To give you a more genuine experience of the nation, Airbnb offers exclusive chances to stay in local homes, apartments, or even traditional Albanian houses.

Eat Albania is an excellent online resource for learning about Albania's delectable cuisine. Authentic eateries, regional food markets, and traditional Albanian specialties are all covered by this website and mobile app. You can find food-related events and trips as well as recipes and information on regional delicacies. For foodies who want to revel in the robust flavors and distinctive gastronomic traditions of Albania, Eat Albania is a terrific companion.

Always keep an eye out for new updates to these websites and apps because they might add new features or improve upon existing ones. With these technological resources at your disposal, you'll have a wealth of knowledge, assistance, and comfort while you discover Albania's treasures, guaranteeing an amazing trip across this alluring Balkan nation.

CONCLUSION

As our trip to Albania draws to a close, it is clear that this vivacious and alluring nation has a lot to offer. Every traveler who is fortunate enough to experience Albania's charms leaves with an indelible impression, from its magnificent landscapes to its rich history and welcoming people. In this final section, we discuss this amazing place and share some final reflections on our experiences.

Albania, a secret treasure tucked away in the center of the Balkans, has changed dramatically in recent years. The nation has remade itself as a popular tourist destination after emerging from a violent past while yet managing to hold onto its unique beauty and cultural history. There is genuine friendliness and openness that greets you as soon as you step foot in Albania and permeates every part of the nation.

The amazing natural beauty of Albania is one of its most notable features. The nation is a haven for nature lovers, from the rough Albanian Alps in the north to the azure waters of the Ionian and Adriatic Seas. Beach lovers can enjoy the country's breathtaking coastline while hikers can explore pristine mountain trails. You will be in awe of Mother Nature's masterpieces when you visit Albania's national parks, like Theth and Valbona.

Another compelling feature of Albania is its lengthy past. Numerous UNESCO World Heritage Sites are located throughout the nation, including the historic city of Berat, the ancient city of Butrint, and the archaeological site of Apollonia. As you meander among historic ruins and take in the inventiveness of earlier civilizations, exploring these locations is like traveling back in time. Your journey will be even more historically rich thanks to the gorgeous mosques and bazaars found in locations like Gjirokastr and Shkodr that bear Ottoman influence.

The Albanian people are unmatched in their friendliness and generosity. They take tremendous satisfaction in introducing guests to their culture, traditions, and cuisine. With its variety of tastes and influences from nearby nations, Albanian cuisine is a wonderful treat for food enthusiasts. As you revel in the cuisine of the nation, be sure to try regional delicacies like qofte (meatballs), byrek (savory pastries), and baklava (sweet pastry).

As with any location, it's crucial to practice appropriate travel habits. Sustainable tourism projects are essential to maintaining Albania's natural beauty and cultural legacy because the country is still under development. You can help the long-term prosperity of this amazing nation by patronizing local companies, participating in your community, and protecting the environment.

Albania is a place that surpasses expectations. Its untamed beauty, extensive history, and welcoming people make it a location you won't soon forget. Albania will capture your heart and leave you craving more, whether you are an adventurer, a history buff, a nature lover, or simply someone looking for an authentic travel experience. Explore your curiosity, acquaint yourself with the colorful culture, and allow Albania to transform you. Your experience here will definitely be filled with learning, awe, and treasured memories that you will remember forever.

Printed in Great Britain
by Amazon

27929468R00079